MW00758138

CULP'S HILL
AT
GETTYSBURG

"The Mountain Trembled..."

By John M. Archer

Ten Roads Publishing

Published by Ten Roads Publishing, LLC.
P.O. Box 3152
Gettysburg, Pennsylvania 17325

© 2011 by John M. Archer
Originally published in 2002 by Thomas Publications

All rights reserved. No part of this publication may be reproduced, stored in a retrieval system, or transmitted, in any form by any means, electronic, mechanical, photocopying, recording, or otherwise, without prior permission of the publisher.

For more information on this title and others please visit our website at: **www.tenroadspublishing.com**

Or contact us via email at:
info@tenroadspublishing.com

ISBN: 978-0-9825275-9-7

First Edition by Ten Roads Publishing
PRINTED AND BOUND IN THE UNITED STATES OF AMERICA

Cover Image "The Attack of Johnson's Division, C.S.A., on Culp's Hill" by Edwin Forbes. Original painting oil on canvas; color transparency courtesy of Library of Congress.

1

CONTENTS

Acknowledgements

My research on Culp's Hill has relied on information and support from a wide range of sources. First and foremost, acknowledgement is due to the long continuum of individuals and organizations, stretching from 1863 to the present day, without whose words this struggle would be but an enigma: the veterans of Gettysburg, whose statements are our best connection to the conflict; the research of Col. John Bachelder, arguably the most dedicated historian of the battle; the records of the Park's overseers, from the Gettysburg Battlefield Memorial Association to the National Park Service; and finally, the present day research of historians like Harry W. Pfanz, William A. Frassanito, and Charles C. Fennell. My appreciation goes as well to the staffs of the Gettysburg National Military Park Library and the U.S. Military History Institute at Carlisle, to Brenda Wetzel at the State Museum of Pennsylvania, to Beverly Bittle for her proofreading skills, and to Licensed Battlefield Guide Clyde James. I have already mentioned historian William Frassanito; additional thanks go to Bill for his friendly advice and material assistance with this book.

There are always those who, knowingly and unknowingly, ultimately make projects such as this come to fruition. Special thanks go to Jim Glessner and Eric Lindblade of Ten Roads Publishing for keeping specialized studies such as this in the public eye. My greatest debt, however, is to my wife Darlene. She has long supported my research, as well as patiently enduring my obsession with the field at Gettysburg. Without her love and understanding, this book would not have been possible.

"The roar of the artillery and rattle of musketry was awfully severe. The mountain trembled under our feet like an aspen leaf..."
- B. A. Jones, 44th Virginia

Preface

In many ways, we have come to view the American Civil War with a bit of nostalgic detachment–representative of a bygone era, a simpler, perhaps more romantic time. And there remains a haunting fascination with the notion of our American family locked in a grim struggle with itself. Gettysburg, as the high water mark of the war, has come to be a mecca for that fascination. Perhaps the most memorable part of a visit there is the view across the wide valley south of the town that, for many, symbolizes the killing fields of a lost generation. However, located less than a mile to the east, the monuments on the heavily wooded slopes of Culp's Hill do not easily lend themselves to visions of long, gallant lines of charging infantry–somehow, something seems to be missing.

In setting out to write this study on Culp's Hill, I began to follow the format of previous projects, interpreting the struggle there by linking veterans' words to the ground where they fought. Yet, I also felt a piece was missing. I often walked the hill with the accounts of those who were there in 1863–expecting somehow to be rewarded with some insight into this strangely muted ground. I just as often found myself oddly unsettled, reminded of author Kent Graham's treatise and the battlefield's whispered admonition, "You don't have it right, and you'll never get it right." Perhaps like the dense woods that cover Culp's Hill, the passage of that generation will always shroud our understanding of what happened there; and a guess would say that generation might find our enduring fascination somewhat odd. For if there is any nostalgic element to Gettysburg, you won't find it on Culp's Hill.

In truth, this largely overlooked ground is reminiscent of elements of war that are all too familiar: trench warfare, overwhelming firepower to devastate the foe, and the horror of "friendly fire." The more I learned about the battle for Culp's Hill, the more I understood some of the uncommon tragedy of that struggle–a distinctively American tragedy, prefaced often by uncommon courage and uncommon sacrifice. The regimental monuments and traces of breastworks that line the crest there bear silent testament to a hellish conflict; no other spot at Gettysburg would see such a sustained period of brutal combat as when North and South vied for this ground.

So, as you follow the course of the battle for Culp's Hill, whether it be in your car or your living room, bear in mind that the struggle described here is only "history" of a bygone era in the sense it deserves remembrance. On this ground, the sacrifice of those who fought here is still very much alive.

John M. Archer
September 28, 2000

Introduction

There is, probably, no place on the Gettysburg battlefield which presents such strong attractions as Culp's Hill. It is natural that the visitor should wish to see some tangible evidence of the battle. Many portions of the field have since been cultivated, and little remains to distinguish them from other and contiguous grounds. But here there is no mistaking the fact that some great and unusual event has occurred.

- Col. John Bachelder, *Gettysburg: What to See, How to See It,* 1873

First designated for preservation in 1863, Culp's Hill joined Cemetery Hill and Little Round Top as the grounds considered most essential for commemorating the battle at Gettysburg. The lines of breastworks and dying groves of shot-riddled trees on its slopes made Culp's Hill a popular stop for early tourists and veterans alike. But even as Bachelder commented on the popularity of the hill in his guidebook, he noted that these scars of war had started to fade. After 1900, even with its trees replanted and eroded defenses rebuilt, Culp's Hill began to lag behind more visually dramatic sites such as the High Water Mark, the Peach Orchard, and Devil's Den. In more recent years, media attention has drawn countless visitors to other areas of the field in search of paranormal activity and motion picture scenarios. It is ironic then, but not surprising, that interest in one of the first areas chosen to memorialize the battle at Gettysburg has declined dramatically.

Today, trees again cover much of the area around Culp's Hill. Yet, the thick foliage covering once open fields and in the historic woodlots themselves makes it difficult to understand the struggle for this area. The monuments that line the avenues on Culp's Hill can tell only a small part of the story; even the accounts of the veterans themselves are in many cases vague, or worse, contradictory. This study is an effort to remedy these obstacles. It is not intended as a comprehensive history of the battle and, for brevity's sake, there is little detailed discussion of individual personalities or unit histories. These areas have been admirably covered in Edwin Coddington's *The Gettysburg Campaign – A Study in Command*, and Harry Pfanz's *Gettysburg – Culp's Hill and Cemetery Hill*. Instead, the reader is invited to tour this seldom explored segment of the battle, using first-hand accounts to help see this ground–much of which has changed little in the past 135 years–with a participant's eye. Maps and photographs are keyed with the text that will help orient those on the field, as well as those unable to visit Gettysburg.

Some of the debates born of hindsight are unavoidable here; a few will be touched upon briefly in the context of the battle *as fought*; others will no doubt occur to the reader. Indeed, several of the contemporary statements presented here are inconsistent; one need only read a few Civil War accounts to realize that combatants rarely agreed in their interpretations of battle. In the course of the text, the author has attempted to suggest a setting that allows these disparate versions to exist side-by-side.

For those who are able to visit Gettysburg, the narrative follows a tour format to interpret the fighting on Culp's Hill. For clarity's sake, the route was determined by the chronology of the battle, rather than attempting a linear sequence of stops. The encounter here was perhaps more complex than any at Gettysburg: in addition to the rugged landscape and the sheer duration of the fighting, several places on the hill saw action repeatedly. Not surprisingly, this requires some areas to be traveled more than once to follow the ebb and flow of the struggle across this ground. If patient, the reader will be rewarded with a better understanding of the unique character of the struggle for Culp's Hill and the men who vied for its slopes.

Map Sources

The original maps included with the text are based on information gathered from the 1864 and 1876 Bachelder Map Series, the 1869 Warren Survey Map, and the turn-of-the-century maps produced under Col. E. Cope. Despite the extraordinary efforts of early surveyors to depict the battlefield, these maps all contain inconsistencies and errors. These base maps were combined with contemporary aerial photographs and field research to create the modern and the 1863 versions presented here.

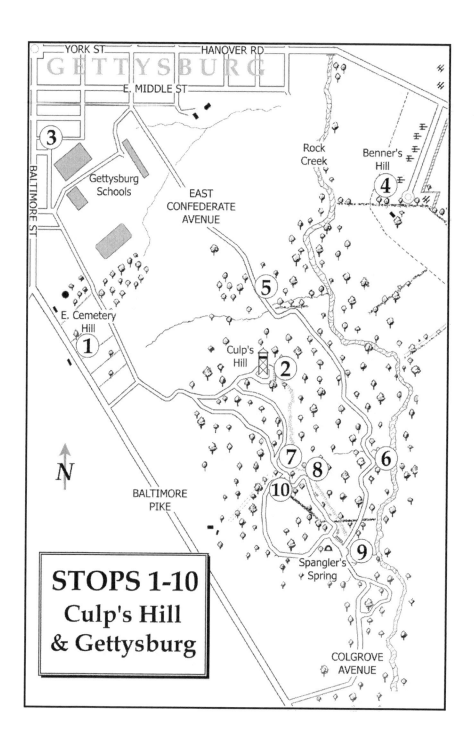

York St · Hanover Rd · GETTYSBURG · E. Middle St · ③ · Baltimore St · Gettysburg Schools · East Confederate Avenue · Rock Creek · Benner's Hill · ④ · ⑤ · E. Cemetery Hill · ① · Culp's Hill · ② · N · ⑦ · ⑧ · ⑥ · ⑩ · Baltimore Pike · ⑨ · Spangler's Spring · Colgrove Avenue

**STOPS 1-10
Culp's Hill
& Gettysburg**

CULP'S HILL AT GETTYSBURG

"The Mountain Trembled"

This study of the battle for Culp's Hill begins with a brief description of the events leading up to the hill's occupation, accompanied by a tour of the surrounding area. For reference, the directions start at the circle at the center of Gettysburg (Rt. 30 & Bus. Rt. 15).

STOP 1: EAST CEMETERY HILL

From the square in Gettysburg, follow Baltimore Street (Bus. Rt. 15 South) and bear left onto the Baltimore Pike (Rt. 97) to East Cemetery Hill. Park your vehicle near the entrance to the National Cemetery. Stay in your vehicle to read the following.

JULY 1

MORNING: "An Affair of Cavalry..."

The morning of July 1, 1863 found the Federal Twelfth Corps on the march to Two Taverns, the Pennsylvania hamlet located midway between Gettysburg and their overnight camp in Littlestown. Arriving shortly before noon, the 9,800 man corps broke ranks onto the slopes along the Baltimore Pike, while the Corps' commander, Maj. Gen. Henry W. Slocum, established his headquarters in the stone buildings that gave the village its name. "The men were asleep or occupied in getting coffee," recalled Capt. Charles Horton, "when we heard, I should think at about one o'clock, the distant sound of cannon in Gettysburg." The rumble of artillery apparently did not arouse too much concern–Federal cavalry had collided with Rebel horsemen the previous evening in nearby Hanover–so the guns were supposed by some to be merely, "an affair of cavalry." 1

In fact, the major role of Northern cavalry in the action was long since over. In a delaying action that began at 8:00

a.m., Union horsemen west of Gettysburg had gradually fallen back before advance elements of the Army of Northern Virginia under Gen. Robert E. Lee. In response to the same orders that brought the Twelfth Corps to Two Taverns, the Federal First Corps under Maj. Gen. John Reynolds arrived on the field at about 10:00 a.m.. Their timely arrival relieved the cavalry and escalated the battle, finally stopping the Southern advance west of the town. As wing commander of the Army of the Potomac, Reynolds was prepared to hold his position outside of Gettysburg until the balance of the Northern forces could arrive. At about 10:30 a.m., however, Reynolds would be killed while leading his men onto the field. 2

In the meantime, riding in advance of his Eleventh Corps, Maj. Gen. Oliver O. Howard arrived in Gettysburg. With the death of Reynolds, seniority placed Howard in command of all the Federal troops on the field. One of Howard's first–and most important–command decisions was to post his reserves on the broad height south of town known as Cemetery Hill.

> After an examination of the general features of the country, I came to the conclusion that the only tenable position for my limited force was the ridge to the southeast of Gettysburg, now so well known as Cemetery Ridge. The highest point at the cemetery commanded every eminence within easy range.... I at once established my headquarters near the cemetery, and on the highest point north of the Baltimore Pike.

Howard ordered the balance of his Eleventh Corps into position north of the town and confronted a new Southern threat from that direction. While the fighting continued to the north and west of the town, the wooded height just to the southeast known as Culp's Hill still held little strategic value; that would soon change. 3

STOP 1 - "The only tenable position..." Howard's headquarters marker on East Cemetery Hill.

Leave your vehicle now and walk to the artillery position on the crest of East Cemetery Hill (south of the Bus Tour parking lot). The up-ended gun tube by the wall on the crest of the hill indicates the location of Maj. Gen. Howard's field headquarters on July 1. Facing back toward the parking lot, you can see the town of Gettysburg to the north and beyond that, the fields of the first day's battle. Over your right shoulder, the wooded height to the southeast is Culp's Hill. Bear in mind that the vista from this spot was considerably more open in 1863, allowing Howard an unobstructed view of much of the terrain surrounding the town.

AFTERNOON: "Not Even a Skirmisher to Meet It"

At 1:00 p.m., Howard sent messages to the two closest Union Corps, the Third near Emmitsburg, Maryland, and Slocum's Twelfth at Two Taverns. In the dispatches, Howard described the morning's battle and that a second Confederate corps under Lt. Gen. Richard Ewell was advancing from the north. Oddly, he mentioned neither Reynolds' death, nor requested the reinforcements he desperately needed. 4

Only five miles away in Two Taverns, Slocum probably received Howard's first dispatch between 1:30 and 2:00 p.m.. Despite the terse message, it seems likely a veteran officer such as Slocum would appreciate the predicament of Howard's two corps. But for reasons still unclear today – whether Slocum was truly unaware of the severity of the situation, or as some claimed, was unwilling to assume command of Howard's precarious battle – Slocum would not start his corps for Gettysburg until almost 3:00 p.m.. Any reluctance would soon be resolved by a dispatch from Taneytown: the Army of the Potomac's commander, Maj. Gen. George G. Meade, ordered all Federal Corps to rush to Gettysburg. 5

By 4:00 p.m., the Northern fortunes had turned. The positions of Howard's beleaguered First and Eleventh Corps were flanked and overwhelmed by the larger Confederate force. Remnants of exhausted Blue regiments streamed back through Gettysburg and were rallied on the high ground to the south around the town cemetery. Located on the flank of this shaky Union position, Culp's Hill now gained significance to both armies.

On the heels of the retreating Yankees, Lee's jubilant Southerners swept into Gettysburg. Pursuing the shattered Eleventh Corps, one of Ewell's Gray brigades under Col. Isaac E. Avery circled to the east of Gettysburg, placing themselves on the flank of the retreating Federals. Skirting

Culp's Hill as it appeared from East Cemetery Hill shortly after the battle. (GNMP)

the buildings on the edge of town, the 1,200 North Carolinians advanced south across the Henry Culp farm by the Hanover Road. Still busy patching together a defensive line on East Cemetery Hill, Federal officers watched with concern. "A line of battle with skirmishers out was plainly seen east of town," observed one, "making its way towards Culp's Hill, and so far as I could see we had not even a skirmisher to meet it." 6

If you were here late on the afternoon of July 1, 1863, the area around you would be in chaos, filled with disorganized Northern units reforming after their defeat. Obscured today by the modern woodlot to your right front (northeast), Avery's Confederates could be seen advancing across the Culp Farm only 1/2 mile to the east.

Across the Baltimore Pike to your left, stands the entrance to Evergreen Cemetery with its distinctive brick gatehouse.

Constructed seven years before the battle, the gatehouse stood prominently on the hilltop in 1863 and became the centerpiece for the new Federal line on Cemetery Hill. Follow the path toward the gate and stop by the cannon there. About five miles down the Baltimore Pike is the village of Two Taverns where Slocum's Twelfth Corps was camped. To your left, note the knoll in front of Culp's Hill; this area will be discussed in the following section.

Fortunately for the Federals, help had arrived on Cemetery Hill in the form of the commander of the Second Corps, Maj. Gen. Winfield Scott Hancock. Learning of Reynolds' death about midday, Meade directed Hancock to proceed to Gettysburg, take command of the troops there, and determine if the situation warranted further concentration of the Army. Arriving near 4:30 p.m., Hancock met Howard near the Cemetery gatehouse, and informed him of Meade's special instructions. Whether Howard would come to appreciate it or not, Hancock's leadership and dynamic presence would prove invaluable in helping forge a new Federal position. 7

Climbing Baltimore Pike from the jam of troops and vehicles at the edge of town, Capt. Greenleaf Stevens' 5th Maine, Battery E, pulled up near the gatehouse, and halted to await orders. Spotting the six Napoleons, Hancock pointed to Culp's Hill and ordered Stevens to "take (his) battery on to that hill," and "stop the enemy from coming up that ravine." Separating his guns from the chaos atop the hill, Stevens led his battery east to the open knoll between East Cemetery and Culp's Hill. None too soon as it turned out, for the Southern brigade could be seen advancing east of town. "As the battery reached this position," one of the Maine men recalled, "the enemy was sweeping through the village and up across the lowlands in our front." Joined by guns on Cemetery Hill, Stevens' battery opened fire on the Gray ranks. Unsupported by the rest of Early's Division, it is unlikely that Avery's small brigade could have gone much farther on their own, but the Federal gunners had made their

15

point. "Shells from the enemy proving very effective," reported a North Carolina officer, "we were soon halted on the hillside, and the men ordered to lie down." 8

At about the same time, Slocum's Twelfth Corps was approaching the battlefield on the Baltimore Pike. In response to Howard's last dispatch, Slocum sent his First Division under Brig. Gen. Alpheus Williams to seize Benner's Hill, a height located east of the town and on the Federal flank. Continuing toward Gettysburg, on Hancock's order, the Second Division under Brig. Gen. John Geary was sent to reinforce the left of the new First Corps position along Cemetery Ridge. 9

By 5:30 p.m., Hancock and Howard had managed to post an impressive line of defense. Five batteries frowned down from the heights between the Cemetery gate and Culp's Hill alone. In support of Stevens' guns on the knoll, Hancock placed the remnants of the Iron Brigade of the First Corps on the northwestern slope of Culp's Hill. There, the exhausted men began work on the first of a line of breastworks that would shape the outcome of the battle for the Federal right on July 2. 10

EVENING: Ewell Blinks

Following the Southern troops into Gettysburg, Corps commander Lt. Gen. Richard Ewell received orders from Lee to press the attack on Cemetery Hill if he, "could do so to advantage". Riding to high ground at the southern end of town, Ewell and his division commander, Maj. Gen. Jubal Early, took stock of the enemy position.

The enemy had fallen back to a commanding position...and quickly showed a formidable front there. . . I could not bring artillery to bear on it, and all the troops with me were jaded from twelve hours marching and fighting, and I was notified that General Johnson's division (the only one of my corps that had not been engaged) was close to town.

16

Cemetery Hill was not assailable from the town, and I determined, with Johnson's division, to take possession of a wooded hill to my left, on a line with and commanding Cemetery Hill.

Adding to Ewell's dilemma, reports reached him from Brig. Gen. William Smith's brigade of an enemy approach on the York Pike to the east. Acting on similar information, Early had previously dispatched a second brigade to support Smith's men on that flank. Riding back to high ground overlooking the Pike, Ewell found no threat, but as a precaution, left the two brigades in place. Whether the result of garbled reports from the Hanover Road of the Federal advance on Benner's Hill, or merely poor observation, the uncertainty deprived Ewell of two relatively fresh brigades and any opportunity for a timely attack on the new Federal position. 11

Returning to the situation south of town, Ewell dispatched two aides to reconnoiter Culp's Hill. Probably riding out of sight in the low ground along Rock Creek, the pair climbed the east side of Culp's Hill to a spot where they could observe the Federal position. Strangely, although the two probably reached the hill after the Iron Brigade arrived on the northern slope, from their perspective Culp's Hill appeared unoccupied. Based on their report, Ewell would justify his position in front of the commanding height to General Lee, followed by the fateful assumption that Johnson's troops would seize the hill that evening. Justified or not, Richard Ewell had set the stage for the battle at Gettysburg that followed. 12

Culp's Hill is about 800 yards southeast of Cemetery Hill, bounded on the east by Rock Creek, and the southwest by the Baltimore Pike. The hill is actually composed of two heights: the taller standing 180 feet above Rock Creek, and a second crest 100 feet lower than the first, and located some 400 yards to the south across a connecting saddle of ground. When viewed from the town, it was this higher elevation that gained the interest of the Southerners on July 1; the saddle area and the lower crest would gain in significance on the following evening. When you are ready, return to your vehicle for the following section.

NIGHT: Opportunity Lost

Near sunset, Ewell's last division under Maj. Gen. Edward Johnson reached Gettysburg after a 25-mile march from Chambersburg. Halting briefly near the Gettysburg rail station for orders, Johnson's weary brigades then followed the railroad bed eastward out to the York Pike. There they turned east across the George Wolf farm, filing into the fields and low ground north of Benner's Hill near the Hanover Road. To the southwest, the dark outline of Culp's Hill was just visible, "The elevated country which we could see in front of us, and the wooded slopes and fields between us and that ridge were, we knew, in the hands of the enemy. The private soldiers of Johnson's Division had a sort of suspicion that we would be expected to sweep the enemy out of their position the next day." "The men, completely worn out, threw themselves down on the ground to rest," wrote another Marylander, "having their cartridge boxes buckled around them and their arms in their hands." Taking advantage of a full moon, Brig. Gen. Johnson sent his own scouting detail to determine the prospects for occupying the heights to the south. 13

In the time since Ewell's first reconnaissance, much had changed on Culp's Hill. With the arrival of 434 fresh men of the 7th Indiana that evening, the Iron Brigade's front now stretched across the north face of the hill to the summit. The 7th's commander, Col. Ira Grover, ordered the regiment to extend the line of breastworks to the crest, and finding no troops to his right, took the precaution of sending picket details down the eastern slope. 14

If Grover's common vigilance that evening did not spare the Army of the Potomac later defeat, it checked any early

18

advantage for Robert E. Lee's army. For, as one of the Indianans recalled, "It may have been a mere military coincidence – perhaps one or the other or both were mind-readers; certain it was while Col. Grover was looking to the safety of our right...[General Johnson] was also looking that direction with a view to turning our flank and getting in the rear of us before morning, and had also sent out a scouting party." On the dark hillside, Grover's thin picket line surprised a twenty-man contingent from the 25th Virginia, capturing their lieutenant. The balance of the Southern party quickly withdrew and reported to Johnson that "a superior force of the enemy" held the hill. 15

It was now after midnight, and a courier arrived from Ewell ordering Johnson to, "take possession of [Culp's] hill, if he had not already done so." At the same time, Johnson was handed a captured dispatch from the commander of the Federal Fifth Corps, Maj. Gen. George Sykes, addressed to Slocum with the Twelfth Corps. The document indicated that part of Sykes' Corps was only five miles away, approaching Johnson's flank on the Hanover Road. As the dispatch was addressed to Slocum, it was apparent the Twelfth Corps was also somewhere nearby. Johnson sent Ewell's courier back with the unwelcome news that not only were Federal troops holding Culp's Hill, seemingly in force, but that substantial Federal reinforcements were arriving; Johnson would delay any advance until he received further orders. By the time the courier returned at daybreak, Ewell had received orders from Lee to hold his position. The assault on Culp's Hill was to await the arrival of Longstreet's fresh corps and an attack on the Federal left. 16

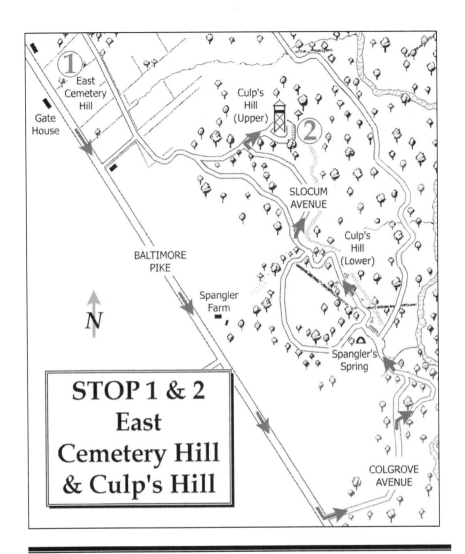

① East Cemetery Hill

Gate House

Culp's Hill (Upper)

②

SLOCUM AVENUE

Culp's Hill (Lower)

BALTIMORE PIKE

Spangler Farm

N

Spangler's Spring

COLGROVE AVENUE

STOP 1 & 2
East
Cemetery Hill
& Culp's Hill

STOP 2 (OPTIONAL): CULP'S HILL, Morning, July 2:
(The following section includes a driving tour on Culp's Hill and a discussion of the Federal occupation of the area early on July 2. You will be returning to this area later, so if you wish to shorten your tour, skip ahead to directions to STOP 3. If you do, read the following text at STOP 4).
To proceed directly to Culp's Hill:
- Go south on the Baltimore Pike for 1 mile past the Cemetery gate.

- *Carefully turn LEFT at the Park signs onto unmarked Colgrove Avenue. [On entering Colgrove Avenue, you may wish to set your trip odometer or take note of your mileage.]*
- *The road will turn right, where it becomes Carman Avenue (.4 miles). In 1863, this area was known as McAllister's Woods, and became the location of the right of the Union Twelfth Corps line.*
- *Bear right from Carman Avenue back onto Colgrove Avenue; pass the Indiana State monument in the clearing, and pause by the parking area on the right. You are now in the area known as Spangler's Meadow. Located to your left, Abraham Spangler's spring had been a popular picnic spot before the Civil War, and early on the morning of July 2, 1863, this was a relatively quiet part of the Federal line. As you will see, this would soon change. For now stay in your vehicle, the tour will return here later.*

Ahead, Slocum Avenue traces the Federal line across the two summits of Culp's Hill. For now, do not stop–you will be able to explore all of this area in a later section. Watch for hazardous curves and possible pedestrian traffic ahead.
- *Leave the parking area and bear right up the hill, following the line of monuments on Slocum Avenue.*
- *After you cross the saddle between the summits, stay to the right on Slocum Avenue.*
- *At the next stop sign (1.1 mile), bear right up the hill and park by the observation tower. The monument for the 7th Indiana (discussed earlier) is on the far side of the circle, and marks the end of the First Corps line. The left of the Twelfth Corps began here and continued down the slope beyond the bronze statue honoring Brig. Gen. George Sears Greene. The actions of Greene and his men would later prove invaluable in the defense of the Culp's Hill.*

Spangler's Spring as it appeared in the 1880's. The modern spring is located in the foreground.

STOP 2 - Monument to Brig. Gen. George S. Greene on the upper crest of Culp's Hill.

JULY 2

MORNING: "We Began to Entrench Ourselves..."

By daybreak on July 2, the Federal position at Gettysburg had been significantly reinforced. In addition to the First, Eleventh, and Twelfth Corps already on the field, nearly all of the Second, Third, and Fifth Corps had arrived, and the Sixth Corps was on the march from Westminster. Meade now arranged his command in a three-mile long arc from Little Round Top to Culp's Hill. Meade initially focused his attentions on the right of his line–if a Southern flank attack seized the Federal lifeline on the Baltimore Pike, the Army of the Potomac would be in dire straits indeed. 1

With the arrival of the Union Third Corps near Little Round Top, Geary's Division moved from its position there to Culp's Hill at about 5:00 a.m.. Similarly, William's First Division was ordered from its overnight post east of Rock Creek into position on Geary's right. Meade then ordered the recently arrived Fifth Corps to the west side of Rock Creek where it would be temporarily under Slocum's command as support for the new Twelfth Corps line. As understood by Slocum, the arrangement now placed him in command of the right "wing" at Gettysburg, and he directed Brig. Gen. Alpheus Williams to step up to command the Twelfth Corps in his stead. Accordingly, as senior officer, Brig. Gen. Thomas Ruger took on command of Williams' division, and Col. Silas Colgrove assumed command of Ruger's brigade. The awkward command structure would eventually create more problems than it solved. 2

On the left of the formidable Blue line that now faced down the eastern slope of Culp's Hill were 1,400 veterans under 63 year-old Brig. Gen. George S. Greene.

We took position at about 6:00 a.m....on the crest of a steep and rocky hill, being thrown back nearly at right angles with the line of the First Corps, Rock Creek running past our front at a distance of 200 to 400 yards. Our position and front were covered with a heavy growth of timber, free from undergrowth, with large ledges projecting above the surface. These rocks and trees offered good cover for marksmen. The surface was very steep on our left, diminishing to a gentle slope on our right...As soon as we were in position, we began to entrench ourselves and throw up breastworks of covering height, of logs, cordwood, stones, and earth. The same was done by the troops on our right.

Facing generally east from the right of the 7th Indiana, Greene positioned his 78th New York on the summit of the hill, followed by the 60th, 102nd, 149th and 137th New York regiments in a line that reached the edge of the low saddle that divided the hill. "It was a bright and pleasant morning when [we] arrived upon the site," observed one of the New Yorkers, "and the soldiers felt restful under the shade of the magnificent trees. While thus resting, an order came through to build breastworks." Under Greene's supervision, the brigade set about constructing defenses for only the second time in their service. Typical of the defenses that took shape on the hillside were those described by Jesse Jones of the 60th New York:

Culp's Hill was covered with woods; so all the materials needful were at our disposal. Right and left the men felled the trees, and blocked them up into a close log fence. Piles of cordwood which lay nearby were quickly appropriated. The sticks, set slanting on end against the outer face of the logs, made an excellent battening.

Other regiments, fortunate enough to have spades and picks, strengthened their position by digging trenches behind the logs, and piling the dirt on the outside of the works. Completed to Greene's satisfaction by noon, a strong line of breastworks ran across the hillside. 3

Greene's breastworks as they appeared within days of the battle. (U.S. Military History Institute)

Modern view of the reconstructed defenses.

At the same time, in the hollow southwest of Greene's line, Col. Charles Candy's 1,800-man brigade formed a support line. Composed of the 5th, 7th, 29th, and 66th Ohio, and the 28th and 147th Pennsylvania, Candy's men stacked arms, and spent the morning resting and assisting Greene's men building defenses. Candy's time on the rear slope would hardly merit notice were it not for a preliminary line of breastworks possibly erected by the 66th Ohio. Incorporating a shelf of boulders on the rear slope, the defenses ran southwest from the right rear of Greene's 137th New York, facing the lower hill and commanding the low ground of the saddle. Soon after, the 109th, 111th, and 29th Pennsylvania regiments of Brig. Gen. Thomas Kane's Second Brigade arrived, extending the front line from Greene's right across the low ground of the saddle to the crest of the lower hill. Commanded that morning by Col. Charles Cobham, these 700 men also set to work fortifying their front line with stones, earth, and fallen timber. Located behind Greene's and Kane's breastworks, Candy's line of defenses was now seemingly useless, but would later prove invaluable. 4

Similarly, the two brigades of William's division formed in two lines on Kane's right. McDougall's 1835-man brigade stretched from the top of the lower hill to its southern slope, with the large 123rd New York and the 46th Pennsylvania in front, and the 3rd Maryland, 145th New York, and 5th and 20th Connecticut in support. With only a regimental front remaining between the right of McDougall's line and the marshy meadow on the south side of the hill, Ruger's 1600-man brigade under Col. Silas Colgrove had a more difficult position to occupy. Colgrove initially placed the 107th New York and the 13th New Jersey on the lower slope. Finding the marshy meadow containing Spangler's Spring to be poor defensive ground, Colgrove placed the balance of the brigade, the 2nd Massachusetts, 3rd Wisconsin, and 27th Indiana some 100 yards to the south in an "irregular square" inside the woodlot of William McAllister. 5

Meanwhile, more Federal reinforcements had arrived on the field in the form of some 1300 men from the defenses of Baltimore under Brig. Gen. Henry Lockwood. Lockwood's 1st Maryland Potomac Home Brigade and the 150th New York arrived at about 8:00 a.m., and reported for assignment to one of the Twelfth Corps divisions. While Williams exercised temporary command of the Corps, the inexperienced Lockwood outranked both acting division commander Ruger, as well as Geary. To keep his divisions in veteran hands, Williams maintained Lockwood's men directly under his command as an "unattached brigade" of the Twelfth Corps. He subsequently placed the two large regiments as supports on the right of Colgrove's line, facing the pond above McAllister's Mill.6

While the Federal position along the crest of Culp's Hill was strengthened, skirmish companies were immediately sent out to probe the Confederate position to the east. Relieving the two companies of the 7th Indiana on the eastern slope, Col. John Redington of Greene's 60th New York led the 170 men of the brigade skirmish companies down the hill and across Rock Creek. In support of Redington's line, Candy's 28th Pennsylvania, 300 strong, followed and formed along the west bank of Rock Creek. As the opposing skirmishers collided, the sound of musket fire increased along the line. "Skirmishing on our left was kept up all day," wrote one New Yorker, "and in the open fields if a man should expose his head to the enemy he would soon hear the whiz of a sharpshooter's ball pass it." 7

By noon, over 8,600 Federals stood behind a solid line of breastworks, stretching from the First Corps line on the north crest of the hill to Spangler's Meadow, and in McAllister's Woods almost half a mile away. With his right secure, Meade began to explore the possibility of an attack from Culp's Hill. Slocum soon dissuaded him–the same terrain features that made Culp's Hill a formidable defensive position rendered it impractical for a Federal offense. The men of the Twelfth Corps settled in to wait what the *afternoon* would bring. 8

You will now be passing through Gettysburg to see Culp's Hill from the Confederate perspective. Before you leave, you may wish to climb the observation tower for an overall view of the area. Use the photos provided to locate the Southern positions around Culp's Hill.
- When you are ready, return to your car and proceed down the hill on Slocum Avenue. On you way, you will pass Stevens Knoll and the position of Federal artillery placed there on July 1 (discussed earlier). Note the earthworks on the right of the road; these indicate the line established by the First Corps on the night of July 1.
- Follow Slocum Avenue to the bottom of Stevens Knoll and turn left at the 33rd Massachusetts monument. Proceed to the stop sign at Baltimore Pike.

STOP 3 - Near the site where Ewell observed the Federal position on July 1. The tower on Culp's Hill is visible to the left; East Cemetery Hill is behind the treeline to the right. In 1863, fence-lined fields stretched from the foreground to the heights.

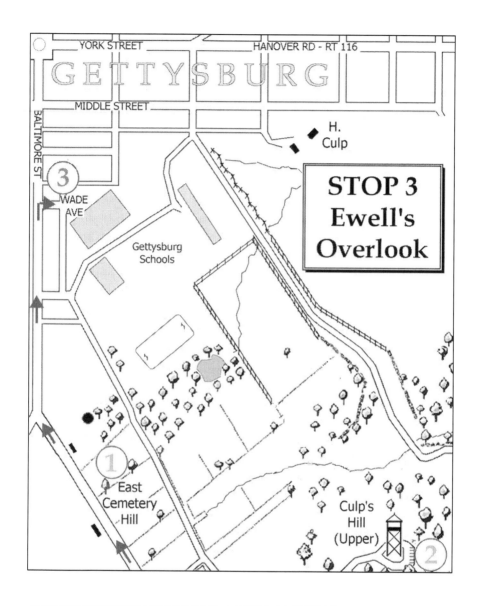

STOP 3: EWELL'S OVERLOOK, *Evening, July 1*
(If you omitted STOP 2, rejoin the driving tour here to view Culp's Hill from the Confederate perspective.)
 - When it is clear, return to Gettysburg on the Baltimore Pike and merge onto Baltimore Street (Bus. Rt. 15).
- Drive .4 mile to Wade Avenue and turn right.

- Park on the right and walk to the intersection with the alley. On the evening of July 1, Confederate Lt. Gen. Ewell probably stood beyond the modern buildings on your left to study the new Union line. In 1863, the low ground to your front and right were open farm fields that stretched to the high ground to the south. Although the area has changed substantially, to your right, East Cemetery Hill is still visible marked by the modern water tank. Beyond the school building in front of you, you may be able to see Culp's Hill and the tower on the summit.

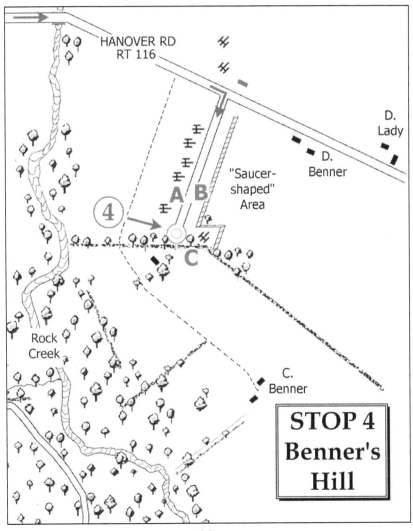

- Turn right and proceed carefully down "Schoolhouse Alley" to the stop sign.
- Turn right at the sign onto Lefever Street to the next stop sign.
- Turn right onto Baltimore Street and proceed .3 mile back to the town square
- Turn right onto York Street (Route 30 East).
- Drive .3 mile to the 2nd light, and go straight at the fork in the road onto Route 116 (Hanover Road).
- Drive .8 mile to the top of the hill and turn right at the sign for Benner's Hill. After turning onto the Park road, if traffic allows, pause briefly on the pavement by the first set of cannon. Visible to your right front, the crest of Culp's Hill stands about 1/2 mile to the southwest. If you look back across the Hanover Road (north), you should be able to see another line of cannon, and beyond the guns, a treeline is visible; this marks the approximate location of the Wolf Farm and the right of Johnson's Division on July 1.

Continue up the Park road to the circle and pull to the right where you will not block traffic. Stay here for the following section.

"This Strange Delay"

Daybreak of July 2 found Johnson's Confederates still in position about a mile northeast of Culp's Hill. The 6,400-man division, consisting of Nicholls', Jones', Steuart's, and Walker's brigades, had formed a long line that reached from the Wolf farm near the York Pike to beyond the Daniel Lady farm on the Hanover Road. At dawn, reinforcements had been sent to the division's picket line, and a strong line of skirmishers began to probe the Federal positions to the east and south. As the day brightened, skirmish fire began to crackle along Walker's front on the Hanover Road and in the valley below Culp's Hill. However, other than minor changes to the division's line, any major action would await developments elsewhere on the field. "It was with something of a feeling of dismay, certainly with one of disappointment," Capt. George Thomas recalled, "that the

31

tired men were roused from their slumbers [that] morning to find the sun high in the heavens and no movement made." 9

Word received from Lee's headquarters now indicated that the main attack was to be by Longstreet's Corps on the Federal left, and Ewell's Corps was to, "make a diversion in their favor, to be converted into a real attack if an opportunity offered." But Longstreet was not in position yet, and by most accounts, Johnson's men chafed at the delay. "Morning passed and noon came, and the men began to ask what this strange delay meant," recounted one, "No more than a mile in their front loomed the hills they were to charge, and sharp and clear rang out the strokes of axes of men felling trees and constructing abatis to obstruct their approach. The latest recruit could perceive that heavy fighting was in store." 10

As morning became afternoon, Johnson's men did their best to pass the time. Those fortunate enough to have shade nearby stayed out of the hot sun; there "they talked in subdued and earnest tones; some of victory ... others of home and the messages they would wish delivered in case of their death." For the introspective, Lt. Randolph McKim of Steuart's staff gave religious services to members of Steuart's Brigade:

> There was a peculiar solemnity in thus appealing to the Almighty for His protection on the field itself, just before rushing forward to assault the lines of the enemy. The men were lying on their arms, momentarily expecting to be ordered to the charge, and they seemed thankful for the opportunity of joining in divine worship. It was for many a poor fellow his last service on earth. 11

At about 10:00 a.m., Johnson ordered Maj. William Goldsborough, a Marylander familiar with the region, to reconnoiter the area around the broad, wheat-covered height between the lines known as Benner's Hill. On receiving Goldsborough's report that "the coast was clear," Maj. Gen.

Johnson rode to the hill himself, accompanied by Goldsborough and artillerist Maj. Joseph W. Latimer. Although Culp's Hill was screened by trees, the group could clearly see Cemetery Hill, and "innumerable batteries of artillery, and immediately in rear of them a long dark mass of infantry, their bayonets glittering in the sun." 12

Any attack on the Federal right would rely heavily on the success of Ewell's artillery in neutralizing the Federal guns massed on Cemetery Hill. Although some support would come from batteries on Seminary Ridge, the principal responsibility for the bombardment rested on the shoulders of Maj. Latimer. Commanding Johnson's divisional artillery in place of the wounded Lt. Col. R. Snowden Andrews, the nineteen-year-old former V.M.I. student was a favorite of the Southern officer corps for his dedication and skill. Latimer had also spent the early morning hours of July 2 searching east of Gettysburg for an artillery platform for his four batteries, eventually settling on Benner's Hill as the only viable location. For most of the day, Latimer kept his Battalion out of sight–although the Federal right was an easy target some 1400 yards to the southwest, Latimer was certainly aware that the Federal artillery also commanded the open crest of Benner's Hill. 13

AFTERNOON: "A Storm of Iron Hail..."

The relative calm ended just after 4:00 p.m.. With the rumble of artillery to the south announcing Longstreet's assault on the Federal left, Latimer's four batteries raced up the slope and unlimbered. Along the crest south of the Hanover Road, Latimer placed his smaller guns–a mixture of smoothbore Napoleons, rifled Parrott guns, and Ordnance pieces–fourteen guns in all. On the knoll to the north of the road, Latimer placed his pair of heavier twenty-pound Parrott guns joining Graham's Virginia Battery of four heavy guns sent earlier from Dance's Battalion. From Seminary

Ridge to the west of Gettysburg, and Benner's Hill to the east, a converging fire arced into the Federal positions across the face of Cemetery Hill. "The shots came thick and fast," one veteran recalled, "bursting, crushing and ploughing, a mighty storm of iron hail, a most determined and terrible effort of the enemy to cripple and destroy the guns upon the hill." 1

Although little fire was initially directed at his division on Culp's Hill, Geary saw that artillery fire from the height would enfilade the Southerners, and ordered guns to the crest. One rifled Parrott gun from Knap's Pennsylvania battery unlimbered by the 78th New York and opened fire. Shortly after, the regiment was moved to the rear and trees cleared, and two more of Knap's guns, as well as a pair of Napoleons from Kinzie's 5th U.S. battery, squeezed into the overlook. The enfilading fire quickly drew Southern attentions to Culp's Hill, and answering rounds began to find targets on the crowded hilltop. To replace casualties, members of the nearby 78th and 60th New York volunteered to serve the guns and deliver rounds from the limbers. 2

In the meantime, Johnson ordered Brig. Gen. John M. Jones to advance his 1,500-man brigade across the road to

STOP 4 - Latimer's artillery position on Benner's Hill. East Cemetery Hill is visible to the right of the cannon.

the Daniel Benner farm in support of Latimer's Battalion. As close support for artillery, the 50th Virginia under Lt. Col. L.H. Salyer moved up to the crest, probably forming along the stone wall south of the guns. Like their counterparts on Culp's Hill, the Virginians were soon called upon to replace casualties in the gun crews: Latimer's misgivings about Benner's Hill were justified. 3

On the afternoon of July 2, 1863, Latimer's guns lined the hilltop from your position back to the knoll on the far side of the Hanover Road. Leave your vehicle, and walk up the Park road to the marker for Carpenter's Alleghany Battery (marked "A" on the STOP 4 map). Looking back to the west, you will see the light blue water tank that marks East Cemetery Hill. Depending on the foliage, to the left of the tanks you may be able to see the Cemetery gatehouse marking the center of Wainwright's artillery line. Beyond the treeline on your left, the crest of Culp's Hill is visible.

The Southern artillery had no sooner opened than counter-battery fire from Federal guns began to sail into the exposed position. "At once, as if directed by the command of one man, our (artillery) poured such destructive fire onto the batteries on Benner's Hill," wrote one of the 5th Maine, "Four of their limbers or caissons exploded and their batteries were silenced." Midway down Latimer's line, Carpenter's Alleghany Battery was particularly hard hit, losing almost a third of its ninety-one members and nine horses. Near the Hanover Road, Capt. William Brown of the Chesapeake Artillery had also been badly wounded, one of his Parrott guns disabled, and only two of the remaining pieces still able to maintain fire. 4

Adding to Latimer's woes, the gunners silhouetted on top of Benner's Hill quickly gained the attention of Federal skirmishers. "About 4:00 p.m. the enemy planted a battery on the hill opposite the left of our line," wrote Lt. Col. Redington of the 60th New York, "I sent forward about 25 sharpshooters who opened a brisk fire on the cannoneers." In response to Redington's move, the remaining companies of the 25th Virginia deployed to reinforce its four skirmish companies west of the hill, apparently with little effect. "The enemy four times advanced their skirmishers (once or twice in a double line)," wrote Redington, "but our skirmishers drove them back." 5

Now walk to the wooden fence on the right (east) side of the road (marked "B" on the STOP 4 map). In 1863, the farm in front of you belonged to Daniel Benner; visible farther the Hanover Road, is the Daniel Lady Farm where the right of Johnson's line stood. During the cannonade, the regiments of Jones' brigade stood near the Benner buildings. In front of you, limbers, caissons, and teams of horses belonging to Latimer's guns occupied the now quiet slope. This hillside is the same described in the accounts that follow.

The Benner Farm site and "saucer-shaped" area from Stiles' account.

The uneven artillery contest continued for almost two hours before Latimer requested to be withdrawn from his position. Passing the hillside, Adjutant Robert Stiles was stunned by the damage to Latimer's batteries:

> [The battalion] had been hurled backward, as it were by the very weight and impact of the metal from the position it had occupied on the crest of the ridge into the saucer-shaped depression behind it; and such a scene as it presented–guns dismounted and disabled, carriages splintered and crushed, ammunition chests exploded, limbers upset, wounded horses plunging and kicking, dashing out the brains of men tangled in the harness…

In all, Latimer's Battalion would lose fifty-one men and thirty horses to the fire of the Federal gunners. With Maj. Gen. Johnson's permission, Latimer withdrew his battered sections, leaving two of Dement's Napoleons and Raine's two rifled pieces to support Johnson's attack. Within minutes, the movement of the Gray brigades again drew attention to Benner's Hill. Again the Federal gunners would open on Latimer's position and silence the Southern guns, this time mortally wounding the young Major in the exchange. 6

What opportunity Ewell saw in the afternoon's actions can only be guessed: his major artillery platform had been eliminated, and the Federal right was not only intact, but the strength of the position on Culp's Hill still an unknown. In addition, by the end of Latimer's demonstration at 6:00 p.m., Longstreet's assault had already raged for two hours, and the benefits of further diversion questionable. Yet from Ewell's perspective, there was still time to turn the "diversion" into an attack and he issued orders: Johnson was to attack Culp's Hill, followed by an assault on Cemetery Hill by Early's and Rodes' divisions. 7

*Stone wall on Benner's Hill likely occupied by Jones'
Virginians while they supported Latimer's guns. The Christian
Benner farm is visible beyond the treeline.*

---

*Return to the circle and walk to the fenced-in area on the left. The
cannon here mark the position of Raines' guns and the left of
Latimer's Battalion. In front of the left-hand gun is a short path
leading to the stone wall where the support line of Jones' 50th
Virginia probably stood (marked "C" on the STOP 4 map). Please
respect the private property that lies beyond the wall while you
view the area. Visible through the trees that line the wall is the
crest of Culp's Hill. The farm on your left was owned by Christian
Benner in 1863. During their advance, Johnson's lines stretched
from here to the woodline of Wolf Hill visible beyond the farm.
Stay in this area for the following section.*

"I Saw a Flutter of Battle Flags..."

After the inactivity of most of July 2, at about 6:00 p.m.
the Gray ranks behind Benner's Hill came alive. As the duel
subsided, Jones' 44th, 21st, 48th, and 42nd Virginia moved
up from their support position on the Benner Farm to wall
on the left of their comrades in the 50th Virginia. There they
halted again while the rest of the division formed behind

them. In the fields north of the Hanover Road, "mounted officers [were] seen dashing furiously down the lines from right to left," one of Steuart's' men recalled, "As they pass the men spring to their feet, and quickly form their ranks. We know what it means, and take our places unordered." On the signal, Steuart and Nicholls' brigades advanced south across the road, "preceded by a cloud of skirmishers." 8

Maneuvering the 4,700-man battleline in the 800 yards available between Benner's Hill and the woodline to the east would prove to a challenge. The three brigades advanced across the hill in at least two sections, probably with Jones' regiments in the lead, followed by Nicholls' and Steuart's brigades. Led July 2 by Col. Jesse Williams, Nicholls' 1st, 2nd 10th, 14th, and 15th Louisiana regiments initially held the right flank of the division. To close the gap left by Jones' earlier advance, the 1,100-man brigade began to shift to their left, closing on Steuart's line before heading southwest to arrive behind the left of Jones' brigade. The result, according to J.G. White of the 1st Maryland, was a line that moved forward, "as if on dress parade." "The Confederate line of battle extended as far to the right as the eye could reach," wrote another Marylander. Although written many years after, the view up the long slope from Greene's skirmish line on Rock Creek was unforgettable:

> Soon regiments of infantry began to appear, and, moving forward, formed in line of battle to the left of [Latimer's] guns. Watching these as they came into line through a field glass, and counting the battle flags and intervals in the front line, I calculated that there were eight regiments, and of probably from 400 to 500 muskets in each. In the rear of these, [who were] forming the front line of battle, were two smaller lines of infantry, formed some two or three hundred yards in the rear as supporting columns. On their left flank, as a curtain, were two or more regiments moving by the left flank in files of four.

Then an officer and staff rode along the front line, and must have made some remarks to the men, as I distinctly saw a flutter of battle flags and hats waving in the air, but they were too far away to be heard. Then the whole mass moved out with their arms at a right shoulder-shift, their movement in perfect alignment. 9

If you wish you return to your vehicle for the following section.

With the passage of years, the glory of the moment overshadowed some of its misfortune, for the Confederate advance on Culp's Hill had its share of both. At the outset, Johnson's left flank unit, the "Stonewall" brigade under Brig. Gen. James A. Walker, was still heavily engaged with Federal skirmishers in the woods to the east. With evidence of a sizeable Federal threat on the Hanover Road, Johnson had given Walker discretion to remain as long as necessary and follow the division as soon as possible; the division was advancing without these 1,300 men. 10

"I saw a flutter of battle flags…" Modern view of the Benner farm from the position of Federal skirmishers at Rock Creek

To the west of Walker's line, Steuart's brigade now formed the left of the advance on Culp's Hill. However, as Brig. Gen. Steuart described: "The hill...lay in a southwesterly direction from our position, and accordingly our left wing was obliged to swing around by a right half-wheel, and the brigade thus formed front toward the west by south." As they crossed the fields east of the Benner farm, Steuart's 2,100-man brigade line consisted of the 10th, 23rd, and 37th Virginia regiments, the 1st Maryland Battalion, and the 3rd North Carolina regiment; the 1st North Carolina followed in a support line, probably on the left just behind the 10th Virginia. On the inside of the wheel, the North Carolina and Maryland men on the right had a relatively short distance to pivot. "[We] were ordered to connect our right with the left of Nicholls' (La.) Brigade, and at the same time by wheel to the right to properly prolong their lines," remembered one Tarheel, "We did so, thereby in some degree disconnecting our regiment from the rest of the brigade." On the outside of the wheel, the left regiments not only had farther to travel, but the 23rd and 10th Virginia were slowed by the tangle of boulders and trees as the brigade passed the north slope of Wolf Hill. In the eyes of Brig. Gen. Steuart, his left flank units had not understood the order and began to lag behind. Whatever the reason, a gap opened between the regiments on the left, and the 3rd North Carolina and 1st Maryland on their right that would have dire results. 11

On the right of the advance, the movement of Jones' regiments across the Christian Benner farm had attracted the attention of Federal gunners on Cemetery Hill. "The head of a column of infantry appeared, crossing Rock Creek immediately in our front," wrote Lt. Charles Brockway of Ricketts' 1st Pennsylvania Battery, "We soon broke the column, compelling those on this side to run behind Culp's Hill for cover, while the main body made a long circuit by a house on their left." On the right of Jones' line, the 25th

Virginia somehow managed to escape harm from the Federal shells; to their left, the 50th and 42nd Virginia were less fortunate. "A temporary halt was made at the foot of the mountain, where the regiment suffered some from the enemy's shells, which had been harmless until the creek was reached." 12

STOP 5: EAST CONFEDERATE AVENUE
When you are ready, drive back along the Park road to the intersection with the Hanover Road. Use caution: approaching traffic is difficult to see and may travel at high speeds.
- When it is clear, turn left.
- Go .6 mile and turn left onto Third Street to the stop sign at East Middle Street. To your left front is the Henry Culp farm, now maintained by the National Park Service; in 1863, Culp's property extended from here to the hill that bears his name.
- Turn right onto East Middle Street, drive one block to the stop sign at Liberty Street.
- Turn left at the stop sign *(It will be helpful to set your trip odometer or note your mileage here).
- Bear to the left and enter the Park on Confederate Avenue (also known as East Confederate Avenue).
- Drive past the school buildings to the top of the rise (.25 mile), and stop briefly in the turnout on the right. In 1863, this area was the edge of the orchard that extended northward to the Culp buildings. The water tank visible beyond the trees to your right marks East Cemetery Hill. Although altered dramatically with the school construction, the knoll behind you is the "hillside" where Avery's brigade hid from Federal artillery fire on July 1. To your left, the crest of Benner's Hill is behind the treeline on the horizon. Culp's Hill lies beyond the small knoll in front of you.
You will now be following Confederate Avenue and the line of Johnson's advance. Note that the road ahead has several blind curves; please watch for vehicles behind you and pedestrian traffic.

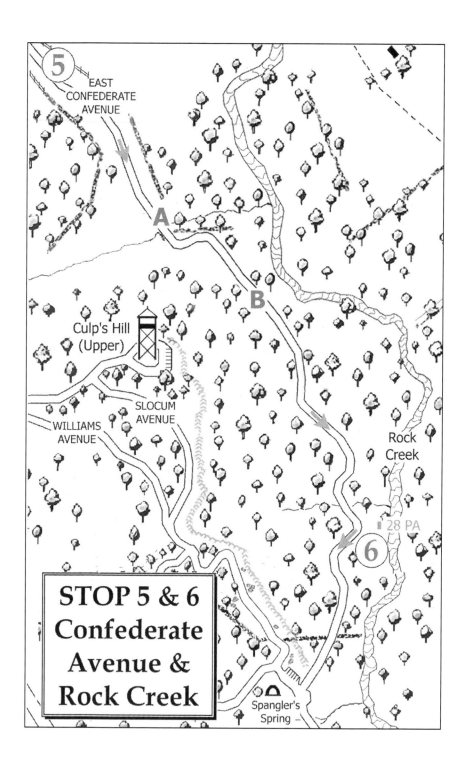

EAST
CONFEDERATE
AVENUE

A

B

Culp's Hill
(Upper)

SLOCUM
AVENUE

WILLIAMS
AVENUE

Rock
Creek

28 PA

6

STOP 5 & 6
Confederate
Avenue &
Rock Creek

Spangler's
Spring

- At .6 mile is the marker for Jones' Brigade (marked "A" on the Stop 5 Map). Stop briefly on the pavement to the right so you do not block traffic. During their attack, Jones' Virginians advanced from Rock Creek to your left, and climbed the steep hillside to your right before attacking the northern summit of Culp's Hill above. In early battlefield records, the wall to your left was described as "Jones' Breastworks," and may well have served as ready-made defenses later in the battle.

- Continue on Confederate Avenue. If the foliage allows, you may be able to see Rock Creek and a pipe-rail fence through the trees to your left. This fence was erected about 1902 by the Battlefield Commission to mark the borders of their land. At .8 mile is the marker for Nicholls' Brigade (marked "B" on the Stop 5 Map). Staying on the pavement, pull to the right side of the road for the following section. Although not as steep as the hill in Jones' front, the boulders and uneven ground around you had to be crossed by Nicholls' Louisianans in their advance toward the crest to your right.

EVENING: "One Blazing Line of Musketry..."

The sun was well behind Culp's Hill when Johnson's skirmishers reached the scattered trees along Rock Creek; there they clashed with their counterparts from Greene's brigade. After offering brief resistance on the east bank, the thin line of New Yorkers fell back across the creek, where they began the fight in earnest. As Lt. Col. Reddington wrote soon after:

At about 7 p.m. they began the advance with their line of battle. I immediately withdrew my line to this side of the brook, and threw forward every man of my reserve. We held this point with the briskest fire we could concentrate. Their line of battle was seen to lie down in the grass. 1

In the Confederate ranks, the casualties began to mount: "Scarcely had we reached the creek that runs by the foot of the mountain when we were fired upon by the enemy who were 'ambushed' nearby, recalled one Southerner, "Four of Co. B fell wounded and many others along the line." On reaching the banks of Rock Creek, the right of Johnson's long line began to wade across the waist-high waters. Once on the west bank, the Rebels reformed quickly and pushed into the woods ahead. 2

After the relatively smooth ground on the Benner farm, the terrain now faced by Jones' and Nicholls' men could hardly have been more different. The crest of Culp's Hill, so prominent on the horizon at the outset of the advance, was now concealed in a boulder-studded woods crossed at intervals by shelves of rock and low bogs; in the growing darkness, the neat ranks gave way to ragged lines and separated regiments. Upon crossing the creek, the right of

Johnson's right flank faced the rugged eastern slope of Culp's Hill. The tower on the crest is visible at the center of the photo.

Jones' brigade faced a steep slope leading to the crest; the left of the brigade had to cross a rocky knoll into a wide wooded basin at the foot of an even steeper climb. As they converged on the height, the ranks of the Virginia regiments began to overlap and became badly disorganized. Brig. Gen. Jones reformed his lines as much as possible in the murk, and the brigades pressed on. 3

STOP 6: ROCK CREEK, Afternoon, July 2:
Continue along Confederate Avenue. To your left, you will see markers for O'Neal's and Daniels' Brigades; these units took part later in the battle and are included in the discussion of July 3.
- At 1.1 mile, you will see the marker for Steuart's brigade. Continue past the marker out of the curve for about 50 yards, and stop in a safe spot on the pavement to the right so your car is visible, but will not block traffic.
- Walk back to Steuart's marker and proceed down the path behind the plaque. At the bottom of the path is the 28th Pennsylvania monument, marking the position of the Federal skirmish reserve on July 2. Just beyond the marker, follow the path to the bank of Rock Creek. The Blue skirmishers who occupied the ground here would recall a somewhat different picture than the low stream with the overgrown banks that you see. At the time of the battle, Rock Creek was blocked downstream by the dam at McAllister's Mill, and the water here stood four to six feet deep. On the far bank, a rail fence stood along the creek, and beyond stood a large cornfield. To your left and front (northeast), Johnson's advancing battle line would be clearly visible as they crossed the open fields of the Benner farm.

Along the banks of Rock Creek, Greene's skirmishers held their ground as long as possible. Sgt. M.L. Olmsted of the 102nd New York recalled:

> *As soon as the advance skirmish line came within reach of us we opened a brisk fire upon it, and the two lines of deployed men were soon battered into one blazing line of musketry...The oncoming line of Confederate infantry halted from time to time, waiting for its advance to clear*

the way, while we in the heavy timber made every tree and rock a veritable battlefield, and probably during the whole war a more stubborn skirmish fight was never waged. Our movements were directed by the bugle calls of a Major in the 60th New York, which rang clear and distinct above the rage of conflict. The smoke of the battle gathering under the dense foliage of the trees, together with the dusk of the evening, soon brought out to view the flashes of the musketry, and so near us came the solid line of battle at one time that its tramp, tramp, and the sharp short commands of its officers became clearly audible. 4

"We advanced across a mill-trail..." Modern view of the road trace leading from the Benner Farm to Rock Creek.

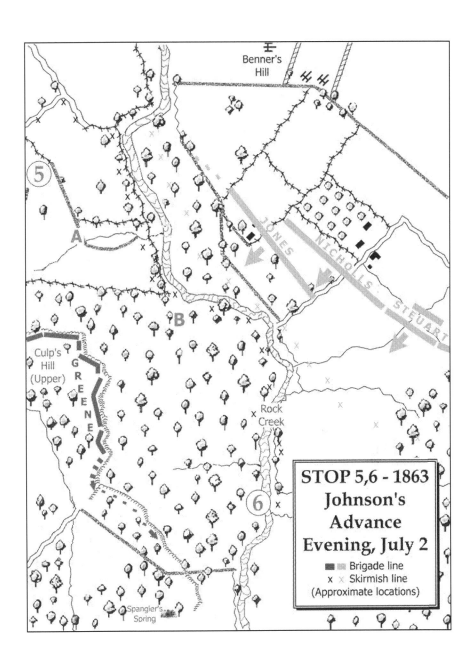

Benner's
Hill

STOP 5,6 - 1863
Johnson's
Advance
Evening, July 2

███ ██ Brigade line
x x Skirmish line
(Approximate locations)

Culp's
Hill
(Upper)

GREENE

Rock
Creek

Spangler's
Spring

JONES

NICHOLLS

STEUART

STOP 6 - The 28th Pennsylvania monument. The turn-of-the-century Battlefield Commission fence beyond borders Rock creek.

On the left of the advance, Steuart's battle line closed in behind their skirmishers, and the fighting grew more heated. One Marylander later wrote:

> *Our skirmishers exchanged shots with those of the enemy, and drove them across the creek into the woods beyond. From the cover thus gained, they fired into our main line advancing over the cornfield, where the corn, being scarcely knee high, did not interfere with their aim. While climbing the rail fence that skirted the creek, Chas. Lloyd and Sam Hamilton were wounded, and in crossing the creek–in some places waist deep–Jas. Ready was killed, or was more probably wounded and then drowned. There was no time to look for crossings; wherever each one happened to strike the water, there he crossed. Once upon the southern bank, the boys raised the Confederate yell and dashed into the woods.*

Anticipating the main enemy line lay somewhere ahead, the 1st Maryland, and presumably other regiments,

"More and more difficult became the ascent..." Terrain west of Rock Creek crossed by Steuart's brigade.

withdrew their skirmishers from their field of fire before they moved on. 5

In the meantime, the difficult crossing had further widened the gap in Steuart's battle line. Anxious to reconnect the brigade, Brig. Gen. Steuart ordered his left regiments to perform a right oblique, shifting the course of their advance toward the rest of the line. As seen by a New York skirmisher, "The main line of the enemy entering the wood at right angles with our line of defense swung its left around so as to become parallel with ours, and came at us with a rush." 6

Without the natural barrier of Rock Creek to slow the Southern advance, Lt. Col. Redington knew time was running out for his thin line. Changes in the Federal line behind him made this fact all the more apparent:

> *I desired to hold a line about 100 yards this side of the brook and sweep them as they crossed the brook. I sent back to the commander of the Twenty-eighth Pennsylvania,*

which had been sent out as a reserve, asking him to move up to that line. He returned answer that he had been ordered to return to the entrenchments. I therefore fell back slowly with my 170 men, contesting every inch of ground, the enemy close on our heels and firing occasional volleys at us. The darkness was so great in this part of the woods that we could not see the enemy, and we fired at the flashes of their guns. They were so close to us that we took 12 prisoners. 7

Still ahead of the rest of Steuart's brigade, the 3rd North Carolina and 1st Maryland Battalion advanced on Nicholls' left through the boulders and swampy ground leading to the lower crest:

Darkness was upon us, and nothing could be seen save the flash of an occasional musket in our front. More and more difficult became the ascent, but over every obstacle pressed the devoted division. Not a shot was now heard, and the woods seemed inhabited but by ourselves. What has become of the enemy?

If Johnson's men had formed any impression of the Federal defenses on Culp's Hill before their advance, a very different situation awaited them in the darkness ahead. 8

Now return to your vehicle. As you walk up the footpath, you may well be in the footsteps of Steuart's Marylanders, who long remembered the shelves of rock and woods that surround you. As you drive, you will be seeing markers for Walker's and Smith's Brigades; these units will also be covered with the discussion of July 3.

51

- Continue along Confederate Avenue. At mile 1.2, when traffic allows, pause by the stone wall; probably built when the meadow beyond was cleared, the wall bisects the lower part of Culp's Hill and marks the former borders of the Abraham Spangler farm. Although unmarked today, "Spangler's Wall" would come to play a significant role in the struggle for this area. For now continue driving, you will return here later.

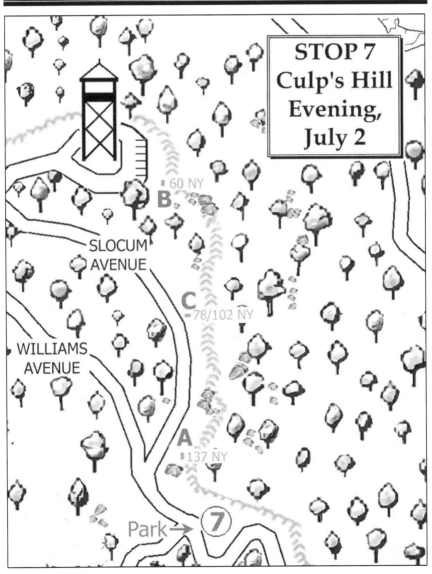

- *At 1.3 mile, turn right at the stop sign and drive past the parking area*
- *Bear right up the hill, following the line of monuments on Slocum Avenue. Watch for hazardous curves and possible pedestrian traffic ahead.*
- *At mile 1.6 is the saddle connecting the two summits of Culp's Hill. Park at the bottom on the gravel to the right. Remain here for the following section.*

"Send All You Can Spare..."

In the time since Latimer's cannonade, the defenses around Culp's Hill had changed dramatically. By 6:00 p.m., Longstreet's attack on Meade's left had crushed the Federal Third Corps line west of Cemetery Ridge. To shore up the position, Meade pulled the Fifth Corps from Slocum's right and portions of the Second Corps from Cemetery Ridge. The piecemeal defense began to collapse and the Confederate advance now threatened to pierce the Union center. Unaware of the pending threat to his right, Meade next sent to Slocum for reinforcements from the Twelfth Corps. For those on the slopes of Culp's Hill, the move was met with justifiable concern. Brig. Gen. Williams wrote in 1865:

> *I received an order from Gen. Slocum to send a division to reinforce the left of our army, which was reported as being hard pressed. Lockwood and the 1st Division being nearest to the line of march, I ordered both to move out around the base of Power's Hill...and I immediately reported to Gen. Slocum that I had great fear that the rebels would seize our line on the right the moment we left it; that I had ordered Geary to cover the whole line and thought we could not safely spare more of our troops from that position. Gen. Slocum said the call for troops was urgent for all the troops he could spare, but he approved of my suggestions that at least one division was necessary to hold our*

entrenchments. With this understanding, I joined the head
of the reinforcing column. 8

With well over half of his corps headed away at the double-quick, Slocum sent an aide to Meade with the recommendation that Geary's 3,900 men stay in position to defend Culp's Hill. For Meade, the immediate point of crisis was on the Federal left, and the aide returned with orders: keep a brigade, but send the balance of Geary's division. "At 7:00 p.m. I received orders to move the division by the right flank and follow the First Division," Geary reported, "leaving one brigade to occupy the line of works of the entire corps. The First Division had gone nearly half an hour previously..." With no guide, Geary's two brigades would soon lose their way and march a mile down the Baltimore Pike, reaching the Rock Creek bridge before halting. 9

To your right front, a line of monuments is visible on the upper slope. Leave your vehicle and walk up the slope to the large boulder marked with a plaque honoring the 84th New York (their role here is discussed later). About 50 paces farther up the slope, locate the monument for Greene's right flank regiment, the 137th New York (marked "A" on the Stop 7 Map). The flank markers on either side of the monument approximate the position held by this regiment on the morning of July 2. Stay in this area to read the following.

With seemingly only skirmish activity in their front, for the moment the attention of Greene's men was on the battle behind them. "From the left, Sickles' position, the roar of the conflict was steady and incessant. [We were] in the dim light of these woods, eagerly listening to that combat," recalled one of the New Yorkers, "when suddenly orders were received for the column to move by the right flank and to extend and lengthen its line." With the departure of Geary's men, Brig. Gen. Greene began the task of shifting his 1,400 men to cover a position formerly held by almost 6,400. 10

To defend his right, Greene ordered Col. David Ireland's 137th New York to shift to the breastworks in the now vacant saddle and lower crest. "We were ordered to change our position to the line of works constructed by General Kane's brigade to occupy which we had to form [a] line one man deep. In this position the right of our regiment was entirely unprotected." With less than 400 men, the single rank of the New Yorkers could cover Kane's position, and much of McDougall's, but fully half of Ireland's regiment would lie on the far side of the lower crest–out of sight of the rest of the brigade, and dangerously exposed. 11

On Ireland's left, the 149th New York and, in turn, the 102nd New York began to undouble their lines, filing to their right to cover the open breastworks. A member of the 102nd New York observed, "To cover this distance there was a very thin line, the men being fully a foot apart, in single rank." Further depleting the line, Greene sent the 78th New York from the crest to replace the recently departed 28th Pennsylvania on the skirmish reserve. The regiment filed

STOP 7 – Modern view of the position first occupied by Greene's 137th New York. The regiment would be sent to occupy the lower hill visible in the background.

down to the more gradual slope in front of the 102nd New York, crossed the defenses, and disappeared into the darkening valley below. "The light was dimmed by the dense foliage," wrote one of the 149th New York, "the woods bore a sombre hue, and all was still as death." 12

The situation in Greene's front began to change rapidly. In the midst of the brigade's shift, the sporadic shots from the woods to the east had become more persistent. "Word was brought from the officer in charge of the pickets that the enemy was advancing in heavy force in line of battle," wrote one of the New Yorkers, "The intention was to place the men an arm's-length apart, but, by the time the left of the brigade had fairly undoubled files, the enemy was too near to allow of further arrangements being made." 13

Continue to follow the line of Federal breastworks up the hill. Here you will pass monuments to Greene's 149th New York, and the 78th and 102nd New York. Bear in mind, these monuments approximate their positions early on July 2, not necessarily those occupied after the regiments shifted to the right that evening. As on Confederate Avenue, you will see several other markers here to units that were not here until July 3.

Up the slope to the left is the castle-like monument to the 150th New York. Follow the line of breastworks about 15 yards to the right of this monument until the path meets a set of large boulders incorporated into the defenses. Follow the path as bends to your left around the rocks and then right again. Continue up the hill about 35 paces until you see a flat tablet with a bronze face honoring Company "I" of the 60th New York (marked "B" on the Stop 7 Map). In 1863, the woods here on Culp's Hill were more open than they are today. Face down the slope to read the following.

With pressure increasing on his thin line, Lt. Col. Redington withdrew his skirmishers to within sight of Greene's breastworks. When within 50 yards of the works, Redington decided it was time to clear a field of fire for the anxious ranks on the hill above and ordered his line back to the crest. The 78th New York followed suit, re-crossing the breastworks the way they had come, taking position behind the right of the 102nd New York. Capt. Jesse Jones of the 60th New York watched impatiently from the breastworks up the slope:

In a short time the woods were all flecked with the flashes from the muskets of our skirmishers. Down in the hollow there, at the foot of the slope, you could catch a glimpse now and then, by the blaze of the powder, of our brave boys as they sprang from tree to tree, and sent back defiance to the advancing foe. . . The men restrained their nervous fingers; the hostile guns flamed out against us not fifteen yards in front. Our men from the front were tumbling over the breastwork, and for a breathless moment those behind the breastwork waited. Then out into the night like chain-lightning leaped the zigzag line of fire.

"For a breathless moment those behind the breastwork waited..."
The defenses held by Company "I" of the 60th New York.

Walk up the hill to the main regimental marker for the 60th New York. Here you can get a better view of the Federal position and the challenge faced by Jones' Southerners in assaulting this cliff-like incline. Move to a spot where you can get a clear view down the slope for the following section.

In a telling letter home, Capt. Steuben Coon of the 60th New York later wrote:

Not a shot was fired at them until they got within about 15 rods. Then the order to fire was given (Fire!) and we did fire, and kept firing. If ever men loaded and fired more rapidly than the 60th did on that occasion, I never saw them do it. The rebels yelled like wild Indians and charged upon us on a double quick. 14

NIGHT: "All Was Confusion..."

The order in which Johnson's brigades reached Culp's Hill is debatable; what is clear is that the Rebel advance was halted abruptly only yards from their goal. On the northern summit, the Federal volleys caught many of Jones' men on a nearly vertical slope. "All was confusion and disorder," wrote Capt. T.R. Bucknor of the 44th Virginia, "The works in front of our lines were of a formidable character, and in some places they could scarcely be surmounted without scaling ladders." Another Virginian recalled, "the enemy had [a] ditch further up the hill filled with men firing down on our heads." 1

Those units not pinned to the hillside by gunfire or too shattered to continue, reformed and advanced again, but any momentum gathered by Jones' troops was spent when Jones himself was critically wounded. Gains in front of the northern crest would only be measured in inches and acts of heroism:

When the order was given, just before we fell back, to charge up to the enemy's works, I collected together the only 3 of my men I could find around me and with the flag and about 20 more went up to the works, where the brave flag bearer fell, and my 3 men together with nearly all that went up there. Coming back I discovered the prostrate form of Gen'l Jones and not being able to find any of my command, I thought the best thing I could do would be assist Major White in carrying him off the field. 2

According to one of the New Yorkers in the breastworks above: "They acted bravely, they came as close as they could but very few got within 2 rods of us, those that did never went away again… Well, they retreated in a hurry. Then we heard their wounded groaning and begging for help." One of those wounded, Robert Slaugher of the 44th Virginia, lay close to the Federal defenses calling for water–just a short distance down the slope, his brother William had to listen helplessly. Both would perish on Culp's Hill. 3

After three fruitless assaults in an hour, their ammunition nearly spent, the Virginians were ordered to fall back down the hill. With Brig. Gen. Jones borne from the field, Lt. Col. R.H. Dungan of the 48th Virginia assumed command of the brigade. No doubt seeing the futility of regaining order on the hellish slope, Dungan pulled his exhausted men back across Rock Creek. The Virginians reformed on the far bank, then re-crossed the creek and took position some 300 yards to the northeast of the crest. 4

Now return to the lower part of Greene's line by following the main path down and turning right just below the 60th New York monument. When you reach the 78th and 102nd monument (marked "C" on the Stop 7 Map), stop and face over the breastworks. As on the upper summit, in 1863 the woods here were more open than they are today. Advancing on Jones' left, Nicholls' brigade struck the Union line along this area.

"They could scarcely be surmounted without scaling ladders..."
The slope in front of Greene's 60th New York.

In the meantime, the charge by Nicholls' brigade on the more gradual hillside south of the crest had little more success. Taking advantage of a shelf of rocks just down the slope, the Louisiana regiments had gained a position about 100 yards below the Federal works. From there, they maintained an "incessant fire," and launched a series of attacks on the line above. There is no mention in Federal accounts, but members of the 14th Louisiana may well have temporarily breached the Yankee line in their front: "Three times we charged the breastworks and were repulsed but the fourth time we succeeded, after a heroic struggle and a loss of many men," claimed Capt. Nathan Rawlings, "I was shot in the leg and bayoneted in the left breast. I don't know how I got out of the breastworks, but the next morning I was in the woods with a number of other wounded men." A number of less fortunate Louisianans were captured, including the color bearer of the 14th Louisiana. The struggle on this slope would rage for almost four hours. 5

Nicholls' Confederates took shelter behind these ledges of rock below the 102nd New York.

The line of rocks held by Nicholls' men is still visible at the bottom of the slope below you. Note the large split tree down the slope about 30 yards to your right. This oak tree is said to be one of the few trees that not only witnessed the battle, but also survived the hail of bullets that virtually wiped out most of the grove on this slope of Culp's Hill.

STOP 8: THE SADDLE & LOWER SUMMIT, Evening, July 2
Return to the saddle between the hills. When you reach the monument to the 109th Pennsylvania in the low part of the saddle, turn to your left on the path that crosses the line of breastworks, and walk about 60 paces into the woods (marked "A" on the Stop 8 Map). Turn and face the way you came. As the right of Steuart's brigade advanced up the draw behind you, the 137th New York had just moved into the defenses on your left and front, and the 149th New York into those above the angle to your right. Stay here for the following section.

61

"Battle scarred veteran." Turn-of-the-century view of one of the trees that survived battle damage. (Library of Congress)

"Men Fell Like Autumn Leaves..."

Initially, the attack by Steuart's regiments suffered the same fate as their comrades on the upper hill. Advancing on Nicholls' left, the 3rd North Carolina and 1st Maryland formed the end of the Johnson's line for the moment, and received the brunt of the first volleys as they approached the Yankee line; those in the low ground in front of the angle in the works faced a deadly crossfire. Marylander William Goldsborough described, "Men fell like autumn leaves; but the brave fellows disdained to retreat."

> *The Third North Carolina and [First] Maryland were face to face with the enemy behind a line of log breastworks, and these two regiments received their full fire at a very short range, for, owing to the darkness, the breastworks could not be seen; at the same moment [they] received an enfilading fire from Greene's New York Brigade which was posted in an angle of the works. The balance of Steuart's brigade was on the other side of the ridge and were not exposed to the fire at all.*

STOP 8 - In this valley, Steuart's Southerners were caught in a crossfire from Greene's New Yorkers holding the high ground on each side of the photo.

Already wounded in the arm, the Maryland battalion's commander, Lt. Col. J. R. Herbert, was struck two more times and was pulled from the hillside gravely wounded. Trapped in the low ground in front of the saddle and the lower hill, the two regiments were ordered to lie down and return fire. The men of the 1st Maryland lay only about thirty yards below the breastworks of the 137th New York:

> *It was a mistake, and over eighty men of the Battalion were killed and wounded here within a few minutes. The enemy, protected by their works within which they had now retired, [could not] be reached with effect by the Battalion's return fire. Contradictory orders passed along the line, "Cease firing!" or "Give it to them, boys! " Move here!" or "Move there!" No command could be heard distinctly above the infernal din. 6*

To make matters worse, the 1st North Carolina had left its reserve position near Rock Creek and was advancing up the slope into the murk. Lt. Randolph McKim, hearing the sounds of heavy fighting in their front, convinced Steuart to allow him to bring the Carolinians forward:

> *I led the regiment up the hill, guided only by the flashes of the muskets, until I reached a position abreast of the line on the right. In front, a hundred yards or so, I saw another line of fire, but owing to the thick foliage could not determine whether the musket flashes were firing up or down the hill. Finding that bullets were whistling over our heads, I concluded the force in our front must be the enemy.*

McKim could not have been more wrong. On his order, the regiment opened fire, hitting several of their comrades in front of the Yankee breastworks before they realized their mistake. Friendly fire added to the rapidly growing casualty list. 7

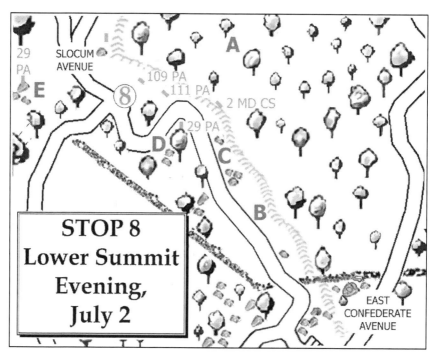

65

Walk back up the path into the saddle. After you cross the breastwork, turn to the left and follow the earthworks up the lower hill. As you pass over the hill, you will see monuments to the 111th Pennsylvania, the 2nd Maryland CSA (1st Battalion), the 29th Pennsylvania, and the 123rd New York.

Continue walking to the south side of the hill until you reach the monument to the 145th New York of McDougall's brigade (marked "B" on the Stop 8 Map). As mentioned earlier, the Federal monuments here indicate positions occupied by these units early on July 2. On the evening of July 2, 1863, the breastworks here–the right end of the Army of the Potomac at Gettysburg–were defended by the single rank of the 137th New York that stretched from the saddle area to this hillside. Turn and face the rocky ledge up the hill for the following text.

Looking north along the defenses held by the right of the 137th New York. Steuart's left breached the Federal line in this area.

Steuart's left regiments–the 10th, 23rd, and 37th Virginia– finally arrived on the southeast side of the lower crest. There Maj. Goldsborough was met by Lt. Col. Simeon Walton of the 23rd Virginia who sought help in attacking the crest. Unaware of Lt. Col. Herbert's wounding, Goldsborough explained he was not in command. Walton shouted over the din, "Well, I shan't wait for orders any longer, but will charge the works if I lose every man in my regiment. Take the responsibility, and charge with your left at the same time." 8

On the slope above with the 137th New York, Col. Ireland realized the Rebel line now extended far beyond his right and would soon envelop his flank. He responded by refusing his line–turning his right company perpendicular to the breastworks to face the new threat. The new line eventually withdrew farther up the hill, probably taking shelter in the large boulders that line the slope there. 9

From the woods below, Walton's Virginians and probably the three left companies of the 1st Maryland charged the lower breastworks. They met little resistance– Goldsborough lost only three men at this point–but there was plenty of gunfire coming from up the slope. Walton wheeled his men to the right, and advancing up the southern slope, encountered another line of troops in the darkness. Whether Walton had learned of the tragic error of the 1st North Carolina or not, he would take no chances. Walton's adjutant, Charles A. Raines, later wrote,

When we gained the earthworks we discovered by the flashes of the guns (it was dark) that these troops (the enemy) were firing in the direction we had come from. The Colonel was puzzled and ordered his men to cease firing and asked for a volunteer to ascertain and report what troops these were. I offered my services and went forward between the two lines to within pistol shot–20 steps–of the enemy...10

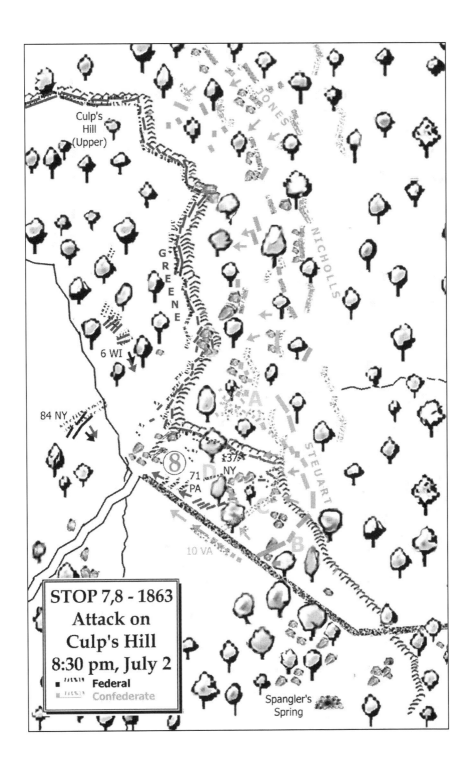

Culp's
Hill
(Upper)

JONES

NICHOLLS

G
R
E
E
N
E

6 WI

84 NY

STEUART

⑧

±37±
NY

71
PA

10 VA

Spangler's
Spring

STOP 7,8 - 1863
Attack on
Culp's Hill
8:30 pm, July 2

■ ▨▨▨ **Federal**
▨▨▨ Confederate

Raines approached a figure on the dark hillside, possibly Sgt. William Cresson of the 137th New York. Cresson, thinking the shots on their flank were coming from McDougall's returning troops, had ventured out from behind a boulder.

> *Sergeant Cresson walked out...and saluting an officer said: "What in h-ll are you doing? Don't you see you are firing into us and will hurt someone?" And when the officer–only a few feet distant inquired what regiment he belonged to and Cresson promptly answered, "137th New York! What troops are you?" And the reply came quick, "Ewell's command." Cresson only had time to spring behind that rock as a pistol bullet whistled by and the officer ran backward towards his men followed by many bullets...*

By this time, Steuart had reinforced Walton's gains, placing the entire left of his brigade in the space between the abandoned breastwork and the stone wall to the west. However, doubts remained about the arrangement of the opposing lines:

> *More...would have been done had not the impression at this time prevailed that we were firing upon our friends, and the fire discontinued at intervals. To ascertain the true state of the case, the Tenth Virginia, under Col. [E.T.H.] Warren (which was on our extreme left, and had formed a line at and perpendicular to the stone wall above referred to), changed front forward along the wall, and then moved by the left flank along it until it was supposed the regiment had gained the enemy's rear...*

Following the path traced by the wall across the dark hillside, Warren's Virginians not only flanked the New York regiment, but also threatened the saddle behind Greene's line. 11

Steuart's regiments crossed the works in this area and turned to face up the slope as you do now. On the slope behind you, a section of Spangler's wall is visible as it continues west into the woods on the far side of the road and disappears to the left of the shelf of boulders. Occupied earlier on July 2 by the support line of the Twelfth Corps, this same wall was used that evening by the 10th Virginia as a guide behind the Yankee line.

Walk back up the hill and stop at the ledge of rocks for the following section (marked "C" on the Stop 8 Map).

"We Found the Breastworks Full of Rebels..."

At last, the besieged Federal right began to receive some much-needed help. In response to requests from Brig. Gen. Greene, regiments from the First, Second and Eleventh Corps began to arrive, and Greene attempted to shore up the endangered points of his line. Possibly prompted by the breakthrough reported by Nicholls' 14th Louisiana, the 147th New York of the First Corps was placed on the left of the 149th New York, where they bolstered the thin line holding the Louisianans at bay. 12

To the embattled lower crest, Greene sent the 71st Pennsylvania from Hancock's Second Corps. No doubt relieved by the addition of 260 men, Col. Ireland pulled the refused right of his line back into the breastworks, allowing the Pennsylvania regiment to move in on his flank instead. As the Pennsylvanians filed into position, they gave a rousing cheer and received volleys from three sides in response. The 71st Pennsylvania would perform creditably elsewhere at Gettysburg, but Culp's Hill was not its finest hour. According to their colonel, Robert Penn Smith, "I engaged the enemy in my front, when he opened on me on my flank and rear. D–n them they had me flanked. It <u>was</u> <u>not</u> my fault. I ordered my regiment to return to a road in my rear–formed my regiment and returned to camp against orders. [I] lost 3 officers and 11 men…" 13

Continue up the hill and cross the road to the 29th Pennsylvania monument. Stand in a spot behind the marker where you look across the saddle (marked "D" on the Stop 8 Map). The line of defenses defended by the 137th New York is across the road to your right. Through the trees to your left, the section of Spangler's wall occupied by the 10th Virginia is visible as it runs into the saddle. The traverse (mentioned earlier and described in the following text) was on the slope across the saddle, and extended from the angle in the breastworks on the right, across the modern avenue, to a point near the single monument in the trees to the left (also a 29th Pennsylvania marker).

Surviving descriptions of the night fighting in this area are understandably confused and frequently contradictory. Although the sequence and exact location of some of the following is unclear, these accounts indicate that the struggle was sudden, chaotic, and desperate.

At about this time, the 6th Wisconsin and the 84th New York (14th Brooklyn Militia), also from the battered First Corps, reached the low area behind the saddle. The Wisconsin regiment under Lt. Col. Rufus Dawes was directed by Greene himself toward a line of breastworks thought to be unoccupied, probably part of the traverse facing the lower hill. Concerned that his men would be silhouetted against the moonlit sky as they crossed the high ground to the rear of the works, Lt. Col. Dawes formed his men into line and ordered them to run silently across the slope.

> *We went up the hill, over the hill, and down the hill without provoking a shot, but we found the breastworks full of rebels. It is hard to tell who was most surprised they or ourselves. But we tumbled the rebels out in less time than it takes to write this. Some of them were of the 10th Virginia Infantry. They retreated down the hill.*

After losing almost half their regiment the day before, the melee cost the 6th Wisconsin another four men, but secured a line of defenses that would prove invaluable in the defense of the hill. 14

Similarly, the 84th New York (14th Brooklyn Militia) also came into line, probably in the low hollow on the right of the 6th Wisconsin. The 84th was greeted with a volley from the Virginians in the treeline near the stone wall. "Fearing from its position in the rear of our line it was our own troops," Col. Edward Fowler wrote, "I sent out a scout who returned and reported it was the 10th Virginia [.] We fired into the woods and silenced its occupants." The New Yorkers' volley may have also temporarily relieved the fire on the 71st Pennsylvania, for shortly after, Smith's Pennsylvanians appeared briefly on the right of the 84th, where they reformed in Spangler's Lane before leaving the field. 15

The departure of the 71st Pennsylvania from the lower crest left Ireland's New Yorkers on their own. Finally confident that those holding the hilltop were the enemy, Steuart's men concentrated their fire on the now exposed line of Yankees. As recalled by Col. Ireland, "At this time we were being fired on heavily from three sides–from the front of the works, from the right, and from a stone wall in our rear. Here we lost severely in killed and wounded." With over a hundred casualties, Ireland ordered the regiment to abandon the hill. Falling back across the saddle, Ireland's men took shelter behind the traverse on the right rear of the 149th New York and reformed facing the lower hill. Abandoned for most of the day, the defenses built that morning now became invaluable in covering Ireland's withdrawal. 16

With the appearance of the First Corps units in the hollow behind them, the 10th Virginia had reformed their line perpendicular to the stone wall, and now opened a punishing oblique fire on Ireland's new position at the traverse. Despite their setbacks and a loss of over a quarter of their men, the 137th New York was far from a beaten unit: "While in this position," wrote Col. Ireland, "Captain Gregg, in command of a small squad of men, charged with the bayonet the enemy that were harassing us the most, and fell, mortally wounded, leading and cheering on his men." The Virginians repulsed the bayonet attack, but the benefits of their position at the wall had obviously evaporated; the Southerners withdrew from the saddle area to rejoin Steuart's men on the lower crest. Soon after, the 137th New York was relieved by Fowler's New Yorkers, allowing Ireland to move his exhausted men behind the hill for a few hours rest. 17

At this point in the battle, the hilltop around you was in Confederate hands. As you look toward the upper hill, compare the view across the saddle to that described in the Confederate account that follows.

"An admirable position…" Today's view toward the upper hill from Steuart's position on the lower summit.

"An Admirable Position..."

It was not yet 10:00 p.m., and the lower summit of Culp's Hill–the right of the Federal line–was in Confederate hands. With the retreat of the 137th New York, the 1st Maryland pushed onto the crest.

> The line chosen by Major Goldsborough for the left of the Battalion was at right angles...within, and some distance from, the captured works, being parallel to the enemy's new line on Culp's Hill proper. Here could be found shelter for his men behind the huge boulders and trees which covered the crest of the hill. Extending west from the summit towards the enemy was a narrow ridge, upon the right slope of which were the captured works occupied by companies A and C...upon the left an open field falling away for about 200 yards to a piece of woods; in front also for a distance of 150 yards the ground was open, and across it ran a stone wall, connecting the hostile lines and perpendicular to both.

To the right of the Marylanders, Steuart's North Carolina regiments connected with Nicholls' line and made the best of the unenviable position in the low ground below Greene's defenses. 18

The long attack and stubborn resistance had taken their toll, for by most accounts, the assault by all three of Johnson's brigades ground to a halt by 10:00 p.m.. Jones' shattered regiments had been reformed 300 yards from upper summit, probably along a stone wall just west of Rock Creek. Nicholls' regiments were able to hold their gains, but lay pinned behind shelves of rock only yards from the Federal defenses; for as one Louisianan recalled, "The night of July 2nd was one never to be forgotten, our lines were so close together that we were compelled to speak in whispers." 19

On the lower summit, Brig. Gen. Steuart and his staff set about trying to determine the benefits of the position they had seized–and at least one of his officers was already aware of their good fortune. After crossing the breastworks and turning to face the fire from the 137th New York, the original western heading of Steuart's regiments had been all but forgotten. Maj. William Goldsborough later wrote:

> That there were no troops in my immediate front I was convinced. Therefore, having acquired some knowledge of the country in my youth, and knowing the Baltimore Pike was but some four or five hundred yards distant, I ordered Captain John W. Torsch to take one of his most reliable men and feel his way in the darkness until he reached the turnpike, unless he encountered the enemy in the meantime. This Captain Torsch did, and reported to me that he had been so close to the turnpike that he was able to see wagons in motion. This satisfied me that we were not only on their flank, but in the rear of the enemy's right. This information I imparted to General Edward Johnson in person a very short time after.

Maj. Gen. Johnson was not given long to consider his options, for the opportunity to seize the Pike, if any, was short-lived. "The reports of scouts and the statements of prisoners gave us the assurance we had gained an admirable position," wrote Brig. Gen. Steuart, "We had been but a short time behind the breastworks when at least two regiments advanced from the woods to the left of the works, and opened fire upon us." The gunfire to the south of the lower crest announced the return of the Federal Twelfth Corps to Culp's Hill. 20

Walk back across the saddle, again heading to the right toward the angle in the defenses. Stop at the boulder with the plaque honoring the 84th New York. Although their marker is located here, it is likely the New York regiment fought on the far side of Slocum Avenue. Incorporating a line of boulders similar to this one, the defenses ran from this point west to the secondary 29th Pennsylvania marker visible across Slocum Avenue. When it is clear, walk across the road to that marker (marked "E" on the Stop 8 Map).

In some respects, this area has changed dramatically in the past 135 years. Many of boulders and ledges of rock that stood here in 1863 are gone, probably used in the construction of the modern road in the 1890's (quarry marks can still be seen on the rocks near where you stand). Access to this area was by Spangler's Lane, the narrow fence-lined path that ran from the Spangler home on Baltimore Pike, diagonally over the ridge beyond the monument, to the low ground in front of you; there it intersected with the stone wall to your left and another fence that extended to the right. (The tour will visit the road trace later). Face toward the saddle for the following.

Modern view looks southwest along the trace of Spangler's Lane visible to the left of the large boulder. Late on July 2, Kane's brigade marched up this narrow lane to reach the saddle.

JULY 2 –JULY 3:

GEARY'S RETURN: "A Night of Bewilderment for All..."

By 9:00 p.m., Slocum's messengers finally located Brig. Gen. Geary on the Baltimore Pike, for at that time Geary ordered Kane's and Candy's brigades to return to Culp's Hill. The roar of musketry from their former position must have concerned Geary's men, but there was apparently little understanding of what had happened in their absence. Leading Kane's 29th, 111th, and 109th Pennsylvania up the Baltimore Pike, Col. George Cobham turned the brigade northeast to cross Spangler's Meadow, presumably expecting to strike the southern end of the Culp's Hill breastworks and follow them to their former position. Entering the woodline on the southern slope, the column was suddenly met with a crashing volley from Steuart's men behind the wall, killing or wounding 14 men in the van of the 29th Pennsylvania. Believing Greene's men had mistakenly fired on his regiment, Col. William Rickards withdrew his Pennsylvanians and rode back to the wall. There he no doubt heatedly explained who he was, but answered by another hail of bullets, withdrew to lead his regiment back to the Pike. With the 111th Pennsylvania in the lead, Cobham continued along the Pike to the Abraham Spangler farm, turning down the narrow lane there to reach the low ground at end of Greene's line. 1

The return of Kane's brigade to Greene's right began one of the more curious episodes in the struggle for Culp's Hill. By this time, Johnson's attacks must have been suspended, and the area relatively quiet, for the Pennsylvanians entered with little caution. Even so, with the chaos surrounding the saddle area just minutes before, it seems incredible there was any question that the Rebel line was nearby, and that no one in Greene's line communicated this information to Cobham's men. Nevertheless, on reaching the saddle, Cobham ordered Lt. Col. Thomas Walker to return the 111th Pennsylvania to their former line of breastworks.

> *I was ordered to place my men in the trenches, and proceeded to do so, under the supposition that there was no enemy in the vicinity. Two companies on the left, which were marching in front, had been placed in position, when we received a volley from the hill, not over 6 rods from our flank and rear. I immediately placed the remaining companies in line perpendicular to the works and facing the direction of the fire we had received.*

At about the same time, a line of skirmishers was sent from the 29th Pennsylvania to determine the extent of Rebel position on the right. Steuart's men allowed the Pennsylvanians to enter their lines before surprising the company captain and five of his men. Seemingly convinced that the Rebels held the lower hill in strength, Cobham placed the 109th Pennsylvania beside the 111th with their right at the stone wall. The 29th Pennsylvania filed behind, their long line eventually stretching from the breastworks into the field beyond the wall. In a compact defensive posture best suited to the darkness and terrain, Cobham placed his regiments four ranks deep, but oddly, did so in the open ground in front of the traverse and directly under Steuart's guns. 2

On the night of July 2, Kane's 700-man formation waited in the darkness on this open ground. The meeting of Kane's officers described in the following took place within a few feet of where you stand.

Finally, at 3:00 a.m. it became evident that the brigade's position was indeed vulnerable, for as Col. Rickards remembered:

> Having observed objects moving in front, Colonel Cobham, Lt. Col. Zulick, and I met in the rear of the center of the brigade to consult, when they opened fire on us, extending entirely across our front, showing them to be in strong force. The fire was returned with spirit by our brigade, and the enemy soon ceased firing, having retreated a short distance behind the crest of the hill. We were then ordered to move back about 50 paces, behind a ledge of rocks.

The Pennsylvanians were moved back to the traverse and adjacent line of boulders, relieving the 6th Wisconsin and 84th New York. There they settled into position, as recalled by Lt. Col. Walker, "awaiting daylight for the work to begin." 3

The return of Candy's brigade to Culp's Hill was curious in a different way. After returning from their fruitless journey out the Baltimore Pike, Candy's men apparently spent much of their time wandering the area west of Culp's Hill. According to one of the 147th Pennsylvania, "It seemed to be a night of bewilderment for all, for I have failed to discover any two members [of the regiment] whose views coincided on the route traversed. It was a night of slow tiresome, round-about maneuvering, through fields, over fences, now on the pike." Finally arriving about 1:00 a.m., the exhausted brigade was initially deployed in the fields behind the Spangler house. Perhaps awaiting Kane's final shifts, even then, Candy's six regiments would not assume their final positions until almost daybreak. At that point, the brigade moved behind Greene's line such that the 28th Pennsylvania, and the 29th and 66th Ohio held support positions in the hollow, while the right of the line, the 5th Ohio, 147th Pennsylvania, and 7th Ohio occupied the area near Spangler's Lane on Kane's right. 4

Before dawn, Maj. Gen. Geary ordered Candy's 66th Ohio to move to the left of Greene's line on the upper crest. Once there, they were to cross the breastworks and, placing their line perpendicular to the defenses, open a flanking fire across the east slope of the hill. In one of the more daring moves of the battle, before dawn, the regiment formed with their right at the works and their left on a pinnacle some 60 yards down the hill; there they would spend the morning firing on the Confederates attacking below and creating an effective crossfire across Greene's front.

To your right, you can see monuments indicating the position of Candy's right regiments along Spangler's Lane on the morning of July 3. The tour will return to this area later.

The 66th Ohio occupied this exposed position on the steep eastern slope of Culp's Hill. Their monument stands above.

STOP 9: SPANGLER'S MEADOW, Morning, July 2-3

[If you wish to walk to Spangler's Meadow, you will need to postpone visiting the position of the 66th Ohio. Skip the directions below and using the maps provided, walk down either Geary or Slocum Avenue to reach the parking lot by Spangler's Spring (see Stop 9 Map).] To drive to Spangler's Meadow:

- Return to your vehicle and again follow Slocum Avenue to the stop sign on the upper summit.

- Turn right towards the tower and park on the summit by the statue of Brig. Gen. Greene. Leave your vehicle and to the left of Greene's statue, you will see two paths leading down the hillside; walk down the <u>left-hand</u> path to the marker for the 66th Ohio just down the slope. As mentioned earlier, the woods here were more open in 1863, allowing the Ohioans a field of fire across

Greene's front to your right, or south. Even today, holding this exposed position seems unthinkable–imagine it without the thicker cover provided by modern foliage.
- Return to your vehicle and proceed back down the hill, following Slocum Avenue to the stop sign at Baltimore Pike.
- When it is clear, turn left, drive .75 of a mile, and again turn left onto Colgrove Avenue.
- At the second stop sign at (.5 miles), continue on Colgrove Avenue across the clearing and park in the parking area on the right (see Stop 9 Map). Stay in this area for the following section.

WILLIAMS' RETURN: "I Deemed it Unwise to Attack..."

Soon after Kane's hasty withdrawal from Spangler's Meadow, Ruger's First Division and Lockwood's brigade also returned to the area southwest of Culp's Hill. During the march back from Cemetery Ridge, Brig. Gen. Williams had been summoned to Meade's headquarters, leaving the reoccupation of the hill in Ruger's hands. At about the same time, Brig. Gen. Ruger learned from one of Slocum's staff officers that Greene's brigade had been left to hold the hill alone, but that Geary's division should have since returned. A more experienced officer than Brig. Gen. Kane, Ruger was understandably suspicious. As McDougall's and Colgrove's brigades reached the Baltimore Pike, Ruger ordered skirmishers sent out to investigate the supposedly empty breastworks. 5

Arriving near Spangler's Meadow at about 10:00 p.m., Colgrove dispatched skirmishers from the 2nd Massachusetts and 27th Indiana to explore the brigade's former position on either side of the swale. On the right, the Indianans found McAllister's Woods clear, and the 27th moved back into the breastworks, followed by the 3rd Wisconsin and 13th New Jersey. Across the meadow to the left, the Massachusetts skirmishers had encountered only one of the enemy. After a second company of Bay-Staters captured another 23 Southerners, Lt. Col. Charles Morse advanced the entire regiment across the swale behind their skirmish line, forming at the end of the breastworks below the lower hill. The 107th New York moved up in support, forming about 50 yards behind and left of the Massachusetts regiment, placing most of their left flank in the woods. Not surprisingly, on further exploration both regiments found a large number of Confederates only a few yards up the hill, and wisely fell back to McAllister's Woods. 6

The position held briefly by the 2nd Massachusetts was at the end of the defenses visible just in front of the modern parking lot. The line of the 107th New York was behind you, and stood about where Spangler's Spring is marked. Only the cover of darkness allowed these regiments to withdraw from a position only yards from the Southern guns just up the slope. Stay by the parking area for the following.

In the meantime, McDougall's brigade had crossed the Pike and formed on the ridge west of McAllister's Woods. Like Kane's brigade, the six regiments were arranged on the knoll there in "double line of battle," a compact formation two regiments deep. Probably shortly after the withdrawal of Colgrove's regiments from the lower hill, the 5th Connecticut and 123rd New York moved down the slope leading to Spangler's Meadow. With orders to move quietly and avoid a night engagement, skirmishers from both regiments probed the woods bordering the meadow. Within minutes, five of the Connecticut men and a New York lieutenant had been seized. As the skirmish lines withdrew, shots were exchanged and the two Blue regiments began to fall back up the slope to rejoin the brigade. Alarmed by the gunfire and the unknown mass of troops moving up the hill towards them, members of the 145th New York opened fire on their comrades. Order was finally restored, but one of the 123rd New York lay dead, probably another victim of friendly fire on Culp's Hill. 7

After the two regiments had settled down, it was apparent Ruger's suspicions had been confirmed:

> I deemed it unwise to attack the enemy, owing to the darkness, the difficult character of the ground, and want of knowledge of the force of the enemy, and immediately placed the division in line along the crest of a slight ridge bordering the swale, with the left of the division advanced from the line, the position best adapted to prevent the enemy from advancing toward the turnpike if he should attempt it, and reported the situation of affairs to Brigadier General Williams, commanding corps.

With the Baltimore Pike secure for the moment, and a new line of pickets guarding their front, Ruger's exhausted brigades lay on their arms for the night. 8

McDougall's skirmishers probably crossed the rocky meadow across Colgrove Avenue between Spangler's Spring and the modern comfort station to the west. There they encountered Steuart's Southerners in the woods that still stand to the right of Geary Avenue. The ridge occupied early on July 3 by McDougall's brigade is visible about 150 yards beyond the rocks, and extends to the west behind the stone comfort station. Stay by the parking area for the following.

Returning from Meade's council at midnight, Brig. Gen. Williams first learned of the precarious situation on Ruger's front. Soon after he conferred with Slocum: "I found Gen. Slocum returning from Gen. Meade, and reported the condition of affairs. His order, was briefly 'Well! Drive them out at daylight.' An order that I then thought was more easily made than executed." 9

Circa 1895 Tipton photo looks southwest across Spangler's Meadow from the wall held by Smith's Brigade. The Baltimore Pike lies in the distance. (Courtesy William A. Frassanito Collection)

Modern appearance of the wall at Spangler's meadow. Spangler's Spring is behind the trees at right center.

JULY 3

MORNING: "The General Plan Was Unchanged..."

General Lee's plans for July 3, at least on paper, were essentially the same as July 2: "The general plan was unchanged. Longstreet, reinforced by Pickett's three brigades...was ordered to attack the next morning, and General Ewell was directed to assail the enemy's right at the same time." As it happened, the execution of these orders could hardly have been further from what was intended. 1

As one of the few concrete gains of the fighting July 2, Johnson's lodgment on Culp's Hill showed promise. "I was ordered to renew my attack at daylight Friday morning, " Ewell wrote in his report, "As Johnson's division was the only one affording hopes of doing this to advantage, he was reinforced by Smith's brigade, of Early's division, and Daniels' and Rodes' (old) division [under O'Neal]." Johnson's lodgment also had drawbacks: merely holding the lower hill held no benefits, and the terrain behind Johnson's line meant that his attack would be without artillery support. But if a brief opportunity existed for the Confederacy the previous evening on Culp's Hill, it had likely disappeared with the return of Ruger's division. Even so, there appears to be little consideration given to a direct assault across the ground leading to the Baltimore Pike. The struggle for Culp's Hill was to continue as a frontal assault in coordination with actions else where on the field. 2

For the time being, in response to the build-up across Spangler's Meadow during the night, Johnson bolstered his flank. Steuart shifted the 1st North Carolina from his right flank to the boulders and stone wall on his left where they could watch the meadow and picket the east side of Rock Creek. Earlier, Walker's "Stonewall" brigade had returned from their position near the Hanover Road, and was placed behind Steuart's line on the crest. Before long, Walker's left flank regiment, the 2nd Virginia, moved up to support the 1st North Carolina. Commanding the Virginians, Col. John Nadenbousch sent another company to the east side of Rock Creek where they joined the North Carolina companies sniping at Colgrove's line inside McAllister's woods. Fresh from their vigil on the York Pike, Smith's brigade of Early's division arrived near dawn, and reinforced the line at the stone wall on Steuart's left. 3

Walk to the line of breastworks visible in front of the parking lot. Follow the line of defenses toward the monuments up the hill to your left until you reach the large boulder incorporated into the works (please avoid walking on the traces). To your right, you will see a path crossing the berm and leading down to more boulders south of the wall (marked "A" on the Stop 9 Map). Follow this path, and on the large boulder supporting the split rock, you may be able to distinguish the initials of A.L. Coble of the 1st North Carolina (see photo); Coble returned here after the war to mark where he fought during the battle. Visible across the meadow is McAllister's Woods, the position of Colgrove's brigade on July 3. Note the excellent cover and field of fire afforded the Southerners who held this side of the meadow.

Just past the boulders, the path heads to East Confederate Avenue. Make your way to the road (depending on the undergrowth, you may wish to return to the parking lot to do so); turn left (north) and proceed up Confederate Avenue to Spangler's Wall and the bronze marker for Smith's Brigade located on your right (marked "B" on the Stop 9 Map). As mentioned previously, the course of the wall formerly crossed where the road is today, continuing east to Rock Creek. Occupied by Smith's Brigade on July 3, the wall marks the left flank of Johnson's line. Like the western section on the crest above, this nondescript section of stones would play a significant role in the struggle for Culp's Hill. Stay in this area for the following.

With first light at about 3:45 a.m., the gunfire reopened across the slopes of Culp's Hill. Maj. Gen. Johnson began preparations to renew his assault on the upper hill with a force twice the size of the previous evening. But the activity

87

along Johnson's line was more than matched by that of the Federals now encircling the lower hill, for as Lt. McKim later observed, "If the Confederates did not realize what they had gained, the Federals were fully aware what they had lost." 4

STOP 9 - Modern view looks south, showing the Confederate field of fire towards Colgrove's regiments. A.L. Coble's initials are carved above the white spot on the lower boulder.

"Drive Them Out at Daylight..."

The Federal plan for the coming morning was straightforward enough: "I made arrangements for a heavy artillery fire, with infantry feints upon the right," reported Brig Gen. Williams, "followed by a strong assault by Geary's division from Greene's position on the left, as I judged would speedily dislodge the enemy." To prevent further attempts to flank the Federal right, Slocum deployed Neill's Sixth Corps brigade south of Wolf Hill on the far side of Rock Creek. Even more critical was the 300-yard gap along the Baltimore Pike between Ruger's and Geary's divisions; there Williams placed Rugg's Battery E, 4th U.S., and Kinzie's Battery K, 5th U.S. Artillery along the knoll west of the Baltimore Pike near the Spangler Farm. As support for the batteries, at about 4:00 a.m. Colgrove's 107th New York and Lockwood's large brigade were placed nearby facing the woods on the lower hill. Combined with Knap's, Winegar's, and Rigby's batteries to the southwest on Power's and McAllister's Hill, over twenty-five Federal guns commanded the ground of Johnson's breakthrough on Culp's Hill. 5

Commencing at 4:30 a.m., a series of barrages by Federal guns announced Williams' intention to retake Culp's Hill. After Johnson's position was pounded for fifteen minutes, the first in a series of uncoordinated infantry "feints" pushed toward the lower hill. Responding to probes by Steuart's brigade toward Candy's exposed flank, Brig. Gen. Lockwood led the 1st Maryland, Potomac Home Brigade, 675-strong, into the woodline west of the lower hill. Within twenty minutes, they had driven Steuart's Confederates back to the stone wall. As he reformed his line for the next charge, Lockwood received word that he endangered an advance by Federals on their left–possibly Geary's proposed charge–and the general ordered a withdrawal. Whether the action of the relatively inexperienced Lockwood was justified, the fruitless effort left 80 Marylanders killed and wounded. 6

Similarly, at about 5:00 a.m. the 20th Connecticut advanced from the left of McDougall's line into the woods west of the lower hill. The body of the regiment halted inside the woodline, and a strong line of skirmishers pushed up the slope where they would hold Steuart's men at bay for some five hours. 7

Retrace your steps down Confederate Avenue and stop at the Indiana monument at the intersection with Colgrove Avenue. Face across the intersection toward the meadow around Spangler's Spring. In 1863, much of the open rocky area in front of you was inside the Culp's Hill woodline. To your left beyond McAllister's Woods were the Federal artillery positions on McAllister's and Power's Hill; on the far side of the modern woods to your right front were the batteries along the Baltimore Pike. When these guns opened fire early on July 3, the converging fire wreaked havoc on Johnson's regiments on the hillside behind you. In the advance that followed, Lockwood's Marylanders advanced almost directly toward your position, and reached the point indicated by the flank markers across the road and on the hill to your right.

Turn left (south) and proceed down Colgrove Avenue (be aware of the two-way traffic here). Walk past the Indiana and Massachusetts monuments that stand at the woodline (marked "C" on the Stop 9 Map), and stop at the large boulder on the right of the road. In front of you is the low ridge occupied by Colgrove's brigade on July 3. (If you wish to explore the ground held by Colgrove's regiments, bear right up Colgrove Avenue and turn left to follow Carman Avenue back to this spot). When you are ready, stand where you can see the meadow. As mentioned, in 1863, the meadow to your left extended back to the Baltimore Pike; the area across Rock Creek to your right was also more open. Stay here for the following section.

The next probe of Johnson's line by Colgrove's brigade would have far more grievous results. Sometime after 5:00

a.m., Brig. Gen. Ruger received orders from Maj. Gen. Slocum to push against Johnson's left at the swale:

> [Maj. Gen. Slocum said] that the enemy were becoming shaky or showed some signs of falling back or some expression of similar import... I reported that I thought the enemy still held that part of the line in force and that any attack would probably not succeed and result in serious loss, and asked that I might first ascertain with certainty that the enemy was still then in force before making the attack, the attack to be conditional on the result obtained. This was approved by General Slocum.

Ruger then sent a staff officer to Colonel Colgrove in McAllister's Woods with orders to advance a skirmish line across the meadow, to be followed by two regiments if Johnson's line appeared weak. 8

Another of the tragic errors in the struggle for Culp's Hill, if Ruger's order was communicated correctly, Col. Colgrove either misunderstood or modified it:

> Between the enemy and our line lay an open meadow, about 100 yards in width. The enemy was entirely sheltered by the breastworks and ledges of rock. It was impossible to send forward skirmishers. The enemy's advantages were such that they would be cut down before they could fairly gain the open ground that intervened. The only possible chance I had was to advance was to carry his position by storming it.

> I selected the Second Massachusetts and Twenty-seventh Indiana for the work, and ordered the Second Massachusetts to charge the works in front of their position; the Twenty-seventh, as soon as they should gain the open ground, to oblique to the right and carry the position held in the ledges of rocks. 9

Receiving the orders for the 2nd Massachusetts, Lt. Col. Charles Mudge commented, "Well, it is murder, but it's the order," and ordered the 316-man regiment across the breastworks. "Without a moment's hesitation and with a cheer, our men sprang over the low breastwork," recalled Charles Morse of the 2nd Massachusetts, "and at a rapid double-quick rushed down the declivity to the edge of the meadow."

> *I doubt if any one of the survivors of that day can clearly describe the crossing of that meadow. At all events I cannot. I know the movement was made very rapidly, and that the fire we passed through was murderous. I also remember how our ranks were thinned as we advanced, but the first thing which is clear to my memory is...after the meadow was crossed.* 10

On your left, the 2nd Massachusetts monument was dedicated in 1879, and was one of the first markers placed on the field. Its location marks the path crossed by the regiment as they advanced north across the meadow. Across the road to your right is the monument of the 27th Indiana, and similarly indicates the path of their charge.

Return up Colgrove Avenue toward the parking area to the Indiana State memorial on your right. Walk behind the monument about 25 yards to the small marker for the following section (marked "D" on the Stop 9 Map).

To Morse's right, the path of the advance by the 27th Indiana was just as harrowing. After maneuvering into position, the 339 Indianans crossed the breastworks just after the 2nd Massachusetts, and angled to the northeast, gradually moving up to the right of Mudge's regiment. As their line became unmasked in the boggy meadow, the Indianans gained the attention of Smith's Confederates sheltered along the boulders and the stone wall southeast of the hill, as well as the Virginians on the Taney farm east of Rock Creek; a telling volley raked the Blue line. A member of Company C, Edmund Brown, later wrote:

It was one of those well-aimed, well-timed volleys which break up and retard a line in spite of itself. Major [Theodore] Colgrove says it appeared to him to knock the three right companies right down... To those who had the whole line in view it almost appeared that a crevasse had opened in the earth and swallowed the regiment, bodily.

Unlike the 2nd Massachusetts who lost no time in crossing the meadow, the Indianans slowed to return fire after crossing the small stream that bisects the meadow. About 100 yards from the Confederate line, the Indiana advance ground to a halt; with the nine-man color guard shot down and his line fading in the withering fire, Lt. Col. John Fesler ordered the regiment to fall back. 11

The advance by the 27th Indiana reached this point in the meadow. Smith's brigade held the treeline in the distance.

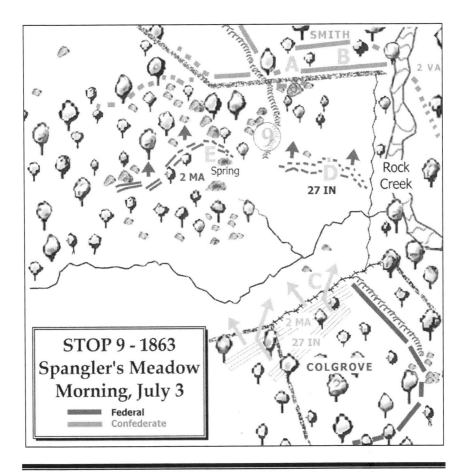

STOP 9 - 1863
Spangler's Meadow
Morning, July 3

Federal
Confederate

As indicated on the marker, this was the farthest point reached by the 27th Indiana in their advance on the Confederate line in front of you.

Now return to Colgrove Avenue, carefully cross the road, and walk to the right toward Spangler's Spring. A few feet past the spring, stop and face the trees at the base of the hill across Geary Avenue (marked "E" on the Stop 9 Map). As mentioned earlier, in 1863 these woods extended into the meadow behind you and across the road to your right. Reaching the shelter of the trees here, the regimental line of 2nd Massachusetts was initially large enough to cover the ground from the rock ledge beside the road to your left to the boulders across Slocum Avenue to your right. Stay here for the following section.

To the left of the battered Indiana line, the advance by the 2nd Massachusetts had reached the base of the lower hill, and Lt. Col. Morse was taking stock of their position:

> The line of the "Second" was brought to a standstill almost against the enemy's breastwork; but here we were somewhat sheltered by rocks and trees, the former rising quite abruptly in front of us... I started toward the right of the line which was suffering more than the left, and near the "color" met Captain Francis and one or two other officers...I looked back over the meadow, and saw a thin rebel line deploying immediately in our rear. This line was under the muskets of our brigade at point blank range, but our friends dared not fire as they could not do so without equal danger to us.

With the withdrawal of the 27th Indiana, Smith's 49th and 52nd Virginia had crossed the wall and charged into the meadow, flanking the New Englanders. "The force...appeared to be a regiment or more," Morse later added, "they were deployed into the swale at a double quick about 50 yards in the rear of the 2nd Massachusetts." Finding that Col. Mudge had fallen, Morse assumed command of the regiment. With his line flanked and a third of his men down, Morse faced the regiment to the rear, and ordered a withdrawal diagonally across the meadow, opening a field of fire on the Rebel line. Reforming at the low stone wall extending west from McAllister's Woods, Morse's men joined the rest of the brigade firing on Smith's Virginians, forcing the Southerners in turn out of the meadow. 12

The cost of Colgrove's errant test of Johnson's flank was high: 112 men of the 27th Indiana lay killed and wounded in Spangler's Meadow, including every member of their color guard. The advance to the base of the hill had cost the 2nd Massachusetts 134 men, including four color-bearers and their commanding officer.

*Circa 1866 view looks north across Spangler's Meadow. The
2nd Massachusetts charged toward Spangler's Spring located
in the treeline. (Library of Congress)*

*"Rising quite abruptly in front of us..." The advance
by the 2nd Massachusetts reached this line of boulders
on the south side of Culp's Hill.*

The ledges of rock that sheltered the 2nd Massachusetts still lie across Geary Avenue and to your right beyond the Park road. Following their withdrawal from Spangler's Meadow, the Massachusetts regiment occupied the stone wall that stands across the meadow to your left rear. Return to your vehicle. (If you walked to Spangler's Spring, follow the directions in the next section on foot).

STOP 10: CULP'S HILL, Morning, July 3
- As you leave the parking lot, turn left (west) to follow Geary Avenue.
- After you pass the comfort station, the road will curve to the right. As described earlier, the 20th Connecticut occupied this area on the morning of July 3 while they contested Steuart's advance in the woods to your right.
- As you continue along Geary Avenue, you will see the monuments to Candy's 147th Pennsylvania and 5th Ohio on your left. (If you are driving, continue to the intersection with Slocum Avenue, park your vehicle at the gravel turnout used for Stops 7 & 8, and return here on foot).

Walk up the hill behind the Ohio monument to the boulder with the oval plaque (marked "A" on the Stop 10 Map). You are now standing in the trace of Spangler's Lane, the path used by many Federal units to reach Culp's Hill. In 1863, the narrow fence-lined path ran from the Spangler home about 300 yards to your left to the low ground to your right where it intersected with Spangler's wall. Turn to face Geary Avenue and what is now known as "Pardee Field" for the following section.

"The Woods Were Full of Them..."

At daybreak, Candy's exhausted regiments northwest of Spangler's Meadow also began applying pressure on the Steuart's foothold on the lower summit. Shifting from their overnight position in the open field northeast of the Spangler farm, the 147th Pennsylvania and 5th Ohio advanced up to a small ridge situated west of Kane's right flank. As recalled by Capt. Joseph Moore of the 147th:

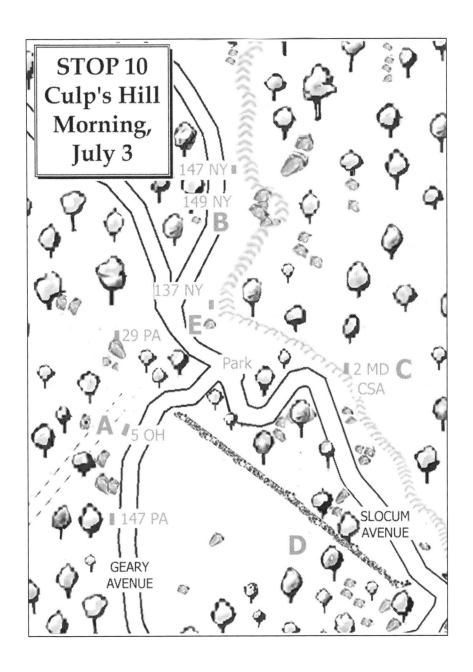

STOP 10
Culp's Hill
Morning,
July 3

147 NY
149 NY
B
137 NY
E
29 PA
Park
2 MD
CSA
C
A 5 OH
147 PA
SLOCUM
AVENUE
D
GEARY
AVENUE

[The regiment faced] a wooded ravine, with an open uncultivated field in the rear. Through the thin skirt of trees in our front was seen a small triangular field, ascending upward from us to a timbered hill beyond. To our left and front, running diagonally to the woods, a stone fence slanted, forming an apex at the woods in which the enemy was posted. ..." We can see no rebs to fire at," said the boys, rubbing their eyes. "Our orders are," replied the commanders of companies, "to keep firing continually and without intermission, through these trees in our front, over that little field and into the woods beyond." It was soon discovered that the woods in question were full of them, for the enemy responded in a lively manner. 13

Soon after, the Blue regiments advanced off the ridge to take advantage of the cover offered by the trees and "ravine" below Spangler's Lane. Although their ranks were relatively unprotected, the shift proved to be a wise one, for as one

STOP 10 - "In our front was seen a small triangular field..."
Pardee Field in front of the 5th Ohio. Steuart's brigade
occupied the treeline at the center of the photo.

Pennsylvanian recalled, "The enemy from his high ground shot over us, causing comparatively light loss on our side, while our fire inflicted great loss to the rebels." To connect with adjacent Federal units, both of Candy's regiments sent skirmish companies to their flanks. On the left, while the main line of the 5th Ohio sent volleys toward the lower hill, a company of skirmishers deployed on their flank to open a crossfire on the lower hill. On the right, Lt. Col. Ario Pardee sent a line of Pennsylvania skirmishers into the woods on their right flank, where they no doubt joined the 20th Connecticut in pressuring Steuart's left. By this time, the musketry from these 600 men composing Candy's right was but a small part of the continuous fire delivered from Geary's front toward Johnson's brigades:

> *The whole line of Geary's Division...kept up a constant fire into the woods directly in front during almost the entire forenoon, and boxes of ammunition were frequently brought up to replenish the cartridge boxes. Occasional silence would ensue, then the enemy would sally out of the cover of the woods and charge upon our line, but the well-aimed rifles of the boys in blue sent leaden hail into his ranks. 14*

Return to Geary Avenue, turn left and walk to the intersection with Slocum Avenue. Turn left again and continue along Slocum Avenue for about 100 yards, bearing to the right as it parallels Greene's defenses on the upper hill. As you walk, note the low ground along Williams Avenue beyond the monuments on your left; this area will be discussed in the following section. To your right, you should see a large rock ledge and the monument to the 149th New York (marked "B" on the Stop 10 Map). Stay in this area for the following for the following.

Circa 1880's view of the position of the 147th Pennsylvania. The ribbons worn by the men in the photo likely indicate they are attending a regimental reunion. (Library of Congress)

Modern appearance of the area shown at top. The tree at center is likely the same as the curved tree in the old photo.

Wintertime view of the ground behind Geary's breastworks. Regiments crossing this ground were exposed to a deadly fire from Confederates on the lower hill (visible through the trees).

"A Wall of Fire..."

With the return of Kane's and Candy's brigades to the south side of the upper hill, Geary's line was again as formidable as the previous day; and unlike the previous night, Greene's exhausted regiments now had relief from a substantial reserve. As the morning progressed, Greene's and Kane's brigades would be relieved by Candy's 28th Pennsylvania, the 7th and 29th Ohio, Lockwood's three large regiments, and eventually, five regiments from Shaler's Brigade of the 6th Corps. 15

The experience of Greene's 149th New York was typical of many regiments occupying the eastern crest. After a short three hours of rest, at daybreak the New Yorkers had returned to their breastworks north of the saddle, and joined the rising crescendo of gunfire.

When the ammunition was nearly expended, the men were ordered to discharge their pieces and fall back on the ground, while the men of another regiment mid deafening cheers leaped over them into their vacant places. Under cover of the fire from the relief, the men made a lively retreat back to the hollow before described amid cheers and exultations... The men were then told to tear their shirts and clean their guns, which were so foul that a ball could not be driven home without difficulty, and the barrels so hot as to be painful to the touch. Fresh ammunition was given the men, but they trusted their work was done. This was a mistake, as the regiment subsequently went into the trenches two or three times...

Repeated by other Northern regiments across the hillside, the result was an unending stream of relatively fresh–and rearmed–Federal soldiers occupying the breastworks. The effect on the attacking Southern lines would be devastating. 16

On the slopes below, Johnson's men returned the relentless fire in kind. Exposed above the breastworks, the flag of the 149th New York would eventually show over eighty holes; its staff, hit several times, was twice shot in two and mended with splints and knapsack straps. Although relatively secure behind their breastworks, the Federals took their share of casualties:

Most of the wounded were injured about the head and upper parts of the body, as the lower extremities were covered by the breastworks. There were those who were injured in the lower limbs. This occurred more frequently when going out or coming into the entrenchments. Most of the companies would average at least one man killed or wounded every time it went in or out.

As the morning wore on, the crisis among the living took precedence over respect for the fallen:

At first the killed were tenderly put back out of the way, but afterwards attention was given only to the wounded unable to get off the field without help. Occasionally the dead were tossed from under foot, but in most instances remained where they fell, and were sat upon by the men while loading their pieces. 17

The sun had not yet cleared the treetops surrounding Culp's Hill, and the next part of Federal plan–the advance by Geary's regiments–was being preempted: "On the discontinuance of the [artillery] fire, the enemy, without waiting our assault, themselves attacked Geary's division with great fury," wrote Brig. Gen. Williams. "The whole line of woods were ablaze with continuous volleys, especially on Geary's front, against which they hurled their columns with a most persistent determination to get possession of the portion of the line held by Greene the night previous." 18

"Mending the Flag" The 149th New York defending Culp's Hill. (Collins, Memoirs of the 149th New York)

"Like Hailstones on a Housetop..."

If they accomplished little else, the Federal probes at Spangler's Meadow had made it clear to Maj. Gen. Edward Johnson that he would have to fight on two battles: one to defend his foothold on the lower summit, the other to attack Geary's position on the upper hill in coordination with Longstreet's assault.

In accordance with Ewell's plan, Daniels' and O'Neal's brigades reached Culp's Hill soon after dawn and went into position east of the upper summit. "I found [Jones'] skirmishers engaging the enemy at long range," wrote Brig. Gen. Daniels, "The hill in front of this position was, in my opinion, so strong that it could not have been carried by any force." Perhaps Johnson's plans had not solidified, or he awaited word of Longstreet's attack; whatever the reason, these two fresh brigades stood in reserve for the next three hours while Johnson's division continued the offensive alone. 19

As the early morning gunfire swelled to a roar, Johnson's assault was renewed "with great determination." But the fruitless charges by Jones' brigade the night before had shown the futility of attacking the upper summit; with the exception of the 25th Virginia, who again occupied the skirmish line, Jones' brigade remained in position near Rock Creek. To their left, Nicholls' regiments still held their position behind the boulders just yards below the Federal works. Hoping to disguise the weakness of their line, the Louisianans opened a heavy fire at daybreak. "When we opened on them, their reply to ours was the most terrific and deafening we ever experienced," wrote one of the 14th Louisiana, "the firing from the overwhelming force in our front became so fierce that our lines were soon enveloped in smoke so we could only see their position by the flashing of their muskets firing." The hail of lead ruled out any withdrawal from the slope, much less further advance. 20

Jones' Brigade in front of the upper summit. (Battles & Leaders)

"Steuart's Brigade renewing the Confederate attack on Culp's Hill, morning of the third day." (Battles & Leaders)

Now retrace your steps down Slocum Avenue, following the road to the lower hill and the 2nd Maryland CSA (1st Battalion) monument (on the left of the avenue at the crest). Walk a few feet behind the monument and stand in a spot where you can see across the saddle for the following section (marked "C" on the Stop 10 Map).

To Nicholls' left, Steuart's position in the captured defenses on the lower summit offered little, if any, advantage. After daybreak, Federal artillery fire from the south and west joined the punishing fire from Geary's regiments on the upper hill. As remembered by one of the 1st Maryland:

> *The whole hillside seemed enveloped in a blaze. Minnie balls pattered upon the breastworks like hailstones on a housetop. Solid shot went crashing through the woods, adding the danger from falling limbs of trees to that from erratic fragments of exploding shells. The whole hill was covered with the smoke and smell of powder. No enemy could be seen. To expose oneself above the breastworks was certain death.*

As during the previous night, the right of Steuart's line suffered the most. "The 3rd North Carolina was almost wiped out, but 19 men being left when morn dawned out of 200." Maj. Goldsborough later wrote, "The two right companies of the [1st] Maryland which adjoined the Carolinians, suffered in as great a number." The pressure on Geary's line probably increased with the advance of Walker's Stonewall Brigade on Steuart's right, but the Virginians above the saddle suffered the same fate as Steuart's men: "[I] became warmly engaged along my whole line," Walker reported, but, "my right extending beyond the breastworks, suffered very heavily." 21

Although not marked as such, it is likely the right of any Confederate line "beyond the breastworks" occupied the small ridge extending east into the woods behind the Maryland monument. Southerners here would be able to enfilade the Yankee line on the higher ground across the saddle, but were dangerously exposed in doing so. Stay in this area for the following section.

The almost continuous gunfire began to take its toll on the Southerners' ammunition, but unlike the Federals on the hill above, few of the Southern units could be pulled from the front line to rest and refit. Beyond what could be gathered from the fallen, ammunition had to be carried from wagons across Rock Creek–in at least one instance, hefted across the water in blankets. 22

Finally ready to press the assault, at about 8:00 a.m. Johnson ordered Daniels to the lower summit. Advancing to the lower hill, Daniels' brigade relieved Walker's Virginians already supporting Steuart, and moved into part of the captured works. Confederate reports of these early attacks is markedly vague; but the scarcity of detail in no way lessens the severity of their struggle. As one of Daniels' 53rd North Carolina wrote in his diary:

> *We were on the brow of one hill, the enemy on the brow of another. We charged on them several times, but of course, running down our hill, and then to get [up to] them was impossible, and every time we attempted it we came back leaving some of our comrades behind... Our regiment was in a very exposed position...and our General Daniels ordered a courier to bring us from the hill. He was killed before he got to us. The general sent another, He was also killed before he reached us. Then General Daniels would not order anyone, but called for volunteers...*

At about this time, Col. Edward O'Neal's Alabama brigade also advanced on Daniels' right, but became pinned in the "murderous fire." Nicholls' Louisianans behind the rocks and trees below the Yankee breastworks began to dread the attempts to support them:

> After the many hours of awful suspense...other of our troops who had not been engaged were sent to relieve us. They came with a yell, but to no other purpose but to intensify a more galling fire in our front. As we looked behind us and saw our comrades coming to relieve us being killed and wounded to no purpose, we regretted that we were being relieved.

By mid-morning, it was plain the Southern attackers faced a far stronger Federal defense than the fragile line of the previous night. 23

"The Worst Was Yet To Come..."

In the meantime, Lt. Gen. Ewell had received more grim news: "Half an hour after Johnson attacked, and when too late too recall him, I received notice that Longstreet would not attack until 10 o'clock." Perhaps it was this information drove Johnson's decision for yet another attack on Geary's line; Steuart's brigade, again supported by Daniels, was to push toward the area between Spangler's Lane and the traverse. The low ground there must have appeared especially vulnerable, for to make the advance, Steuart's regiments would be required to make an unusual maneuver: assemble and attack at a right angle to the breastworks they had defended all morning. Steuart's aide, Lt. Randolph McKim, later remarked: "My diary says that General Steuart and General Daniel, who now came up with his brigade to support the movement, strongly disapproved of making the assault . . . But though [Steuart] remonstrated, he gallantly obeyed the orders he received." 24

With the 10th Virginia pushing the stubborn skirmishers of the 20th Connecticut from the woods west of the stone wall, Steuart's regiments filed into the woodline at the south end of the field fronting the lane. As described by Maj. Goldsborough:

> *Filing to the left, and then to the right, all the companies of the battalion but two crossed a stone fence running parallel with the log breastworks, and about a hundred yards distant. The companies on the left of the stone wall formed on the edge of the woods, but on emerging from its cover had a field to cross without any shelter whatsoever, whilst the two companies on the right of the stone wall were sheltered by woods throughout the whole charge.* 25

[The tour will now follow the path of the advance by Steuart's regiments. If it is inconvenient to follow the "overland" route, you may skip the next directions. Instead, return to the intersection of Geary and Slocum Avenues, walk to the left to where Spangler's wall meets with Geary Avenue, and left again to face "Pardee Field." Stay in this area for the following section; the walk will return there shortly.]

View looks southwest across Spangler's wall. Steuart's regiments formed along this woodline before their charge.

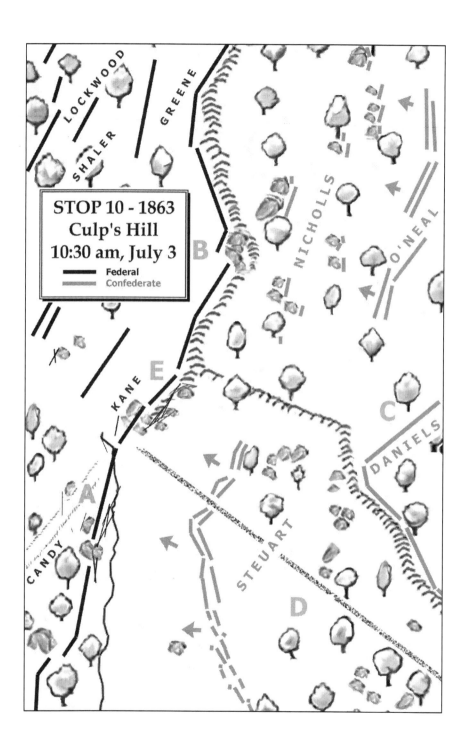

STOP 10 - 1863
Culp's Hill
10:30 am, July 3

Federal
Confederate

To trace the probable route of Steuart's regiments, turn left (south) and follow the line of breastworks to the monument for the 123rd New York (about 25 yards over the crest). Turn right along the line of boulders there, carefully cross the road, and make your way to the stone wall beyond. Carefully cross the wall, and walk into the edge of the woods on your left (marked "D" on the Stop 10 Map), and face the field. Note that, ironically, Steuart's brigade formed with their backs to the Federal position at Spangler's Meadow just beyond the treeline behind you.

Steuart arrayed his line with the 1st North Carolina, 23rd and 37th Virginia, and most of the 1st Maryland Battalion facing the open field, and the right Maryland companies and 3rd North Carolina in the trees between the wall and the breastworks. To their right, Daniels' regiments filed into the now empty defenses with orders to be ready to support the advance. On the right of the Maryland line, D. Ridgely Howard waited with Company A:

> *The movement had been made quietly, the men seeming to feel the solemnity of the occasion, and to understand the desperate nature of the charge to be made: it was a terrible and trying time for all... The order to "Fix bayonets!" was quietly given. All being ready, Gen. Steuart took his position to the rear of my company, and gave the command, "Attention, battalion, forward march!" Just as we started, I heard one of our officers (Lieut. Murray I think,) say, "Use your bayonets boys; don't fire!"—an order I tried to carry out.*

As the brigade entered the field, the vulnerability of the advance was immediately apparent. Commanding the 1st Maryland, Major Goldsborough later wrote:

> *Ten feet of woods intervened before the left companies of the [First] Maryland and the Virginia regiments and First North Carolina came into the field and were exposed to the view of the enemy strongly posted in the woods less than two hundred yards off. The woods uncovered the men of the*

regiments on the left of the [First] Maryland and they threw themselves on the ground, and despite the pleadings and curses of their officers refused to go forward. Never shall I forget the expressions of contempt upon the faces of the left companies of the [First] Maryland as they cast a side glance upon their comrades who had proved recreant in this supreme moment. 26

Keeping the wall to your right, walk about 25 yards to the top of the rise and stop in a spot where you can see the Spangler's Lane trace to your left and the location of the traverse on the upper hill to your right.

With the North Carolina and Virginia regiments on the left faltering, the concentrated Federal fire on the charging ranks of the 1st Maryland and 3rd North Carolina was telling:

View toward Geary's position from the ground crossed by the 1st Maryland. The 5th Ohio marker is visible on the left.

113

As soon as we were unmasked a most terrific fire was opened upon us from three directions. In front, on a rising ground heavily wooded, the enemy were posted in two lines behind breastworks, one above the other, so that both lines could fire on us at once. On the left was a piece of woods, from which the enemy's sharpshooters opened a very galling fire, raking our whole line...

"Still we pressed on until near their breastworks, when, turning my head to the right I saw a sight which was fearful to behold," Pvt. Howard recalled, "It appeared as if my entire company was being swept away by the awful shower of shot and shell flying around us." 27

Continue walking alongside the wall. As you descend the slope here, you are following the path of the center of the 1st Maryland Battalion; as they crossed this area, they received heavy fire from Candy's regiments to your left and Kane's brigade on the slope to your front and right. (If you did not walk the "overland" route, you will rejoin that walk here). When you reach where the stone wall meets Geary Avenue, turn right and walk to the stop sign at Slocum Avenue. Turn left and walk about 50 paces toward the upper hill and stop on the left of the road (marked "E" on the Stop 10 Map). Turn and face across the saddle where you can see Spangler's wall and "Pardee Field." During Steuart's attack in 1863, the slope here was defended by Kane's brigade. Stay in this area for the following account.

On the upper hillside, Kane's 29th and 109th Pennsylvania formed a solid line along the traverse and boulders between Greene's right and the stone wall. At the traverse, Maj. Robert Deckert of the 29th Pennsylvania faced the right of Steuart's line as it came into view:

Our men had been firing at will all the morning, and when the head of the enemy's column appeared in sight, did not need any orders to commence firing. The enemy advanced steadily somewhat covered by the rocks and trees, until they arrived at one hundred paces from our line where the ground was more open. Noticing by the falling leaves that our men were firing too high the colonel gave the command to shoot at their knees, the effect of which was noticeable at once. 28

The sight of the gray ranks charging into the saddle was hard to forget:

Nothing could surpass the regularity with which the enemy advanced, their arms at right shoulder shift, dressing as if on parade to fill the vacancies in their diminishing ranks occasioned by the destructive fire which ploughed into their solid columns. But being right in front the men must have seemed to themselves to be dressing to the left to swerve from our fire. This probably caused the first wavering: their compact quick step was changed to a double quick, and that to a run; finally the foremost men rushed in as best they might upon us. Many continued to advance after receiving their death wounds, falling forward to expire inside our lines... 29

"The enemy came on steadily until within sixty paces when, our fire beginning to tell on them, they began to waver," recalled Maj. Deckert, "At forty paces their confidence failed them." In front of the Yankee lines, the remnants of Steuart's 1st Maryland and 3rd North Carolina were staggered: "[My men reached] within twenty yards of the enemy's works, " wrote one Southerner, "when a volley more destructive than any yet received was poured into them, killing and wounding two-thirds of their number. There was but one thing left for brave men to do...." Lt. McKim later wrote:

The end soon came. We were beaten back to the line from which we had advanced with terrible loss, and in much confusion.... By the strenuous efforts of the officers of the line and of the staff, order was restored, and we reformed in the breastworks from which we had emerged, there to be again exposed to an artillery fire exceeding in violence that of the early morning. 30

Ten years later, Brig. Gen. Kane recalled the attack in a poignant footnote:

[A pet dog] charged with the [Maryland] regiment; ran ahead of them when their progress was arrested, and came in among the boys in Blue... At first, some of my men said, he barked in valorous glee; but I myself first saw him on three legs between our own and the men in Gray on the ground as though looking for a dead master, or seeking on which side he might find an explanation of the tragedy he witnessed, intelligible to his canine comprehension. He licked someone's hand, they said, after he was perfectly riddled. Regarding him as the only Christian minded being on either side, I ordered him to be honorably buried. 31

About 10 paces to the right of the stop sign in the saddle is a small marker. This indicates the farthest point reached by the 1st Maryland Battalion in their charge on the Federal line.

While Steuart's men charged Geary's line here, yet another attack was made on the east slope of Culp's Hill. For this action, return across Slocum Avenue to the line of Greene's defenses. Turn left and follow the line of breastworks up the slope, retracing your steps to the 149th New York monument (marked "B" on the Stop 10 Map). Continue walking about 10 paces farther to the small marker for the 147th New York. Turn and face the slope below the defenses for the following section; as you read, remember the woods here were more open in 1863.

"A Useless Sacrifice of Life..."

To support Steuart's advance, Johnson ordered Walker's Stonewall Brigade to shift from the lower hill and attack on the eastern slope. There, the Virginians advanced shortly after 10:00 a.m. and, as described by Walker, met with "equally bad success." "[We] relieved General Nicholls' brigade," wrote a member of the 5th Virginia, "we were

116

117

"The Repulse of Johnson's Division by General Geary's White Star Division." Painting by Peter F. Rothermel. Detail includes the traverse and shelf of boulders in the foreground, and Maj. Gen. Geary and Spangler's Lane at right. (Courtesy State Museum of Pennsylvania, Pennsylvania Historical & Museum Commission)

Modern view of the area depicted in Rothermel's painting.

hotly engaged for some three-quarters of an hour, under a murderous and enfilading fire. The line on the left began to give way, which was soon followed by the whole line." In the breastworks above, the 7th Ohio took part in the repulse of Walker's attack:

> The enemy formed his line of battle at the foot of the hill and came across the intervening space of woods and rock in splendid order, while we lay behind our solid breastworks, obeying the command to reserve our fire until the first line was well up the slope and in easy range[.] When the command, "Front rank–Ready–Aim low–Fire!," was given and executed, and immediately the rear rank the same, and [this was] kept up as long as the line remained unbroken... When those solid lines of gray were melted away before our volleys...numbers of the enemy [took] refuge behind trees and rocks, and we put in the time while waiting for the next charge sharp-shooting them. A spot of gray showing from behind a tree, or a hat above a rock, was sure to draw the fire of a dozen muskets. 32

Soon, the relentless gunfire from a seemingly impregnable Federal line began to tell. Pieces of white cloth and handkerchiefs began to appear on the hillside in front of the upper hill; unable to advance or retreat, individuals and squads of Southerners began to surrender. One of the largest groups was in front of the 7th Ohio, where Sgt. Lawrence Wilson remembered:

> A white flag was raised, and as soon as it was discovered by Col. William Creighton of the Seventh Ohio Infantry, the order was given to cease firing and the invitation extended to "come in." Up sprang seventy-eight Confederates, many of them members of the Fourth Virginia Infantry, some of them sorely wounded who approached our lines and were welcomed with outstretched hands to a place of safety.

The woods in front of the 78th and 102nd New York.

In an attempt to halt the surrenders and rally the brigade, Maj. Benjamin W. Leigh, Johnson's chief of staff, spurred his horse up the slope. Still in the front line with the 102nd New York, Sgt. Martin Olmsted was one of many who described the episode:

> *A man on horseback was seen flitting along out in the timber in our front, waving a drawn sword and apparently urging forward a line of men. Probably 100 muskets reserved their fire, watching this daring horseman, when all at once he appeared plainly outlined in a small cleared spot, and a score or more muskets rang out in an instant. Both horse and rider went to earth in the twinkling of an eye.* 33

With over a quarter of his force down, Brig. Gen. Walker broke off the attack: "The fire became so destructive that I suffered the brigade to fall back to a more secure position, as it was a useless sacrifice of life to keep them longer under so galling a fire." Walker's exhausted regiments pulled back to Rock Creek.

View up the slope toward Greene's breastworks. Many of Johnson's men became stranded in these rock formations.

Pinned down in front of the breastworks here, the Southerners on this hillside had to choose between almost certain death in a retreat under heavy fire, or surrender. As described in the previous section, Maj. B.W. Leigh charged across the low ground in front of you, and was felled by members of the 7th Ohio and 102nd New York on this slope. On the following day, Brig. Gen. Greene would direct that Leigh be honorably buried near the Federal dead on the crest.

This stop concludes your walking tour of Culp's Hill. If you wish, you may return to your vehicle for the following section. As you leave this hillside, take a moment to remember the steadfast courage of the men who charged these defenses, and the firm resolve of those who held them.

AFTERNOON: "All Had Been Done..."

The failure of the morning assaults–and still further delays in Longstreet's attack–brought Johnson's offensive on Culp's Hill to a halt. "The enemy were too securely entrenched and in too great numbers to be dislodged by the

121

force at my command," wrote Johnson, "No further assault was made; all had been done that was possible to do." After holding the lower summit for over fourteen hours, at midday, Steuart's and Daniels' brigades were withdrawn to Rock Creek. One can only imagine Johnson's chagrin minutes later when the rumble of artillery from Seminary Ridge announced the start of Longstreet's assault. 1

After trading ground with Steuart's men for some five hours, McDougall's 20th Connecticut quickly pushed across the stone wall onto the crest, followed by the rest of McDougall's brigade. In the eyes of these Northerners, it was their advance that drove the Rebels from the hill: "[The 20th Connecticut] opened the way for us and with a shout we charged over the wall," New Yorker L.R. Coy wrote to his wife, "only to see the rebels spring over the breastworks and by the time we reached them they were on a wild run through the woods beyond." "There had been hard fighting here," recalled another New Yorker, "The dead lay on the ground all along the line." 2

The Federals would have little opportunity to relax. Unwilling to relinquish control of the eastern slope, Johnson's skirmish line, as well as Southern sharpshooters posted in trees and behind boulders, continued the galling fire on the Yankees along the crest. To the southeast across Rock Creek, Walker's 2nd Virginia still occupied Wolf Hill, not only keeping Neill's skirmishers at bay, but delivering a punishing fire on the exposed portions of Colgrove's line in McAllister's Woods below. "The house and rocky ledges on the hill beyond the creek, were really somewhat behind us," wrote E.R. Brown of the 27th Indiana, "and the sharpshooters with which they were infested had a raking fire along our line. Had it not been for the timber, our position would have been wholly untenable." 3

With the start of Lee's cannonade at 1:00 p.m., overshot artillery rounds intended for the Northern troops on Cemetery Ridge also began to fall on Culp's Hill. One of the

123rd New York later wrote, "The air seemed filled with iron missiles, and the forest trees were riven, torn, and splintered as if by lightning." Waiting in the hollow behind the defenses on the upper hill, Greene's 149th New York found themselves seeking cover from Rebel bullets from the east and artillery rounds from the west. At the end of the cannonade, McDougall's and Lockwood's brigades would again be sent to reinforce the Union center, but, as on the day previous, were not engaged; however, unlike July 2, they would return to find Culp's Hill securely in Northern hands. 4

Other than intermittent clashes in the dark along the skirmish line, the struggle for Culp's Hill ended at sunset on July 3. Bitter enemies during the day, both sides now shared in their exhaustion. "Darkness put an end to the firing," wrote one Rebel, "The men worn out with hunger and the day's work and excitement, fell asleep." On watch in the breastworks above, one of the 149th New York expressed the same sentiment: "The men tried to keep awake, but it was impossible on account of their excessive fatigue…. The strain on the nerves by the concussion of firearms during the day wearied the body beyond description." 5

After the failure of the afternoon assault, Lee issued orders for Ewell's Corps to retire that night to the army's new line west of Gettysburg. Twenty-four hours after capturing the lower summit of Culp's Hill, Johnson's brigades re-crossed Rock Creek, and silently withdrew to the west.

AFTERMATH

"None But Demons Can Delight in War..."

Early morning probes by Federal pickets on July 4 confirmed suspicions that Johnson had indeed withdrawn from Rock Creek. Word spread quickly along the Federal ranks: "The men were awakened at daybreak to a glorious Fourth of July, with the salutation, 'The enemy has skedaddled, and we are masters of the field.'" Occupied with survival for the previous thirty-six hours, the Northerners began to take stock of their surroundings: "We were a hard-looking set of fellows when the battle was over," penned Sgt. Sam Lusk of the 137th New York, "Our faces were as black as cole [sic]. Our clothes were covered with blood and dirt. Some places in the trenches were saturated with human blood..." 1

"The stillness being oppressive, some dare-devil jumped on the works and crowed in imitation of a rooster, then calling for his rifle, leaped over," one of Candy's 28th Pennsylvania later wrote, "There was no danger—the living foes were gone, the dead alone remained." Tentatively no doubt, others began to explore the slope in front of their defenses:

It was surprising to see the evidence of the terrible character of the Union fire irrespective of the number of dead, which were many hundreds. The trees were stripped of their leaves, and in some instances of their bark. The trunks of trees looked like target boards, and many had not space upon them from the roots to high up in the branches where a man could put his hand and not cover a bullet hole. The ground was covered with flattened bullets, and the rocks were pitted with lead marks.... All over the side-hill were stone piles and little holes dug to cover the enemy while lying on the ground.

But it was the slaughter on the hillside that was appalling, even for Greene's veterans: "The impressions received during that morning walk will never be effaced from memory, " wrote one of the 149th New York, "It made the men sick in body and mind... The havoc in the Union lines was terrible, but among the enemy it was more so." In a letter home, Sgt. L.R. Coy of McDougall's 123rd New York recalled, "In a spot not 12 feet square I saw 8 dead–but I cannot describe what I saw, it was too horrid–truly [I] thought as I passed over the field none but demons can delight in war." 2

Northern details began the grim work of clearing the carnage. "Those of the Union army were carefully put in single graves," wrote G.K. Collins of the 149th New York, "Those of the enemy, with a very few exceptions, were buried indiscriminately in long trenches dug near the spot where they fell." Later, S.R. Norris of the 7th Ohio entered in his diary: "I have just returned from being one of the 'pall bearers' in the largest funeral I ever attended, having been detailed to help bury the rebel dead in front of our brigade; and we dug a trench into which we piled about 200, and carried off 2,000 stand of arms." Twenty-five years later, the scene was still fresh in Norris' mind:

> *As long as reason holds her sway, until all else is forgotten, I shall remember that day and its ghastly dead. We took them from perfect lines of battle as they had fallen; we dragged them out from behind rocks; we found them behind logs or lying over them, with eyes and mouths distended, and faces blackened by mortification. We found them everywhere in our front, from within a few feet of our fortifications to the foot of the hill. 3*

The Confederate losses on Culp's Hill were heavy indeed: of the approximately 6,400 engaged in Johnson's division, the battle for Culp's Hill claimed over 2,000 men killed, wounded, and missing; casualties in the reinforcements from Early and Rodes' divisions would add at least 600 to that total. Engaged almost continuously, Steuart's and Nicholls' brigades suffered the majority of Johnson's casualties, each losing over a third of their number. 4

Although Gettysburg was costly for the Army of the Potomac as well, the defenses on Culp's Hill had proven their worth: of the 9,800 engaged, casualties for the entire Twelfth Corps numbered almost 1,100 men; hard-fought units, such as Greene's 137th New York, and Colgrove's 27th Indiana and 2nd Massachusetts, would bear the brunt of these losses. 5

On July 5, Johnson's Division joined Lee's Army of Northern Virginia in their retreat from Gettysburg. Soon after, the Federal Twelfth Corps left their well-worn defenses on Culp's Hill and started down the Baltimore Pike to join the Army of the Potomac in the cautious pursuit of the Southerners. As each regiment reformed clear of their defenses, the cost of the struggle was more apparent. Written years later, the author of the following could well have fought on either side of the breastworks at Culp's Hill:

As the respective regiments marched out...the losses could be more fully appreciated. Some of the regiments and companies had new commanding officers, and comrades who had been accustomed to march in the ranks and cheer the men with their smiles and jokes were not there.... One regiment was noticed standing by the roadside, which went into the fight at least five hundred strong, but did not now exceed a hundred. The survivors looked sad and mournful, and many eyes in the moving column were filled with tears. 6

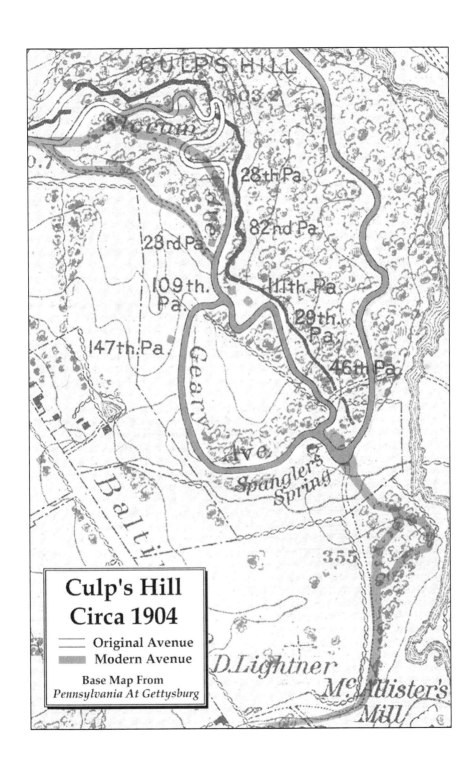

CULP'S HILL

303

Slocum

28th Pa.

82nd Pa.

23rd Pa.

109th. Pa.

111th. Pa.

147th. Pa.

29th. Pa.

46th Pa.

Geary

Ave

Spanglers Spring

Balti

355

**Culp's Hill
Circa 1904**

—— Original Avenue
�▬▬ Modern Avenue

Base Map From
Pennsylvania At Gettysburg

D.Lightner

McAllister's
Mill

APPENDIX

Despite the passage of almost 150 years since the battle for Culp's Hill, the early accounts and photos presented here make it clear that a veteran of that struggle might yet find his way around. As a benchmark, this section will offer a brief overview of some of the more visible changes, as well as features that have since disappeared.

Breastworks

One of the early attractions of the area, the original breastworks that defined the Federal position on Culp's Hill are marked today only by a low earthen berm. But were it not for early preservation efforts, it is unlikely we would see any trace of the formidable defenses that shaped this part of the battle.

By most accounts, the defenses erected on Culp's Hill were based on felled trees and cordwood, supplanted by rocks and dirt. With the departure of the antagonists, the Culp and Spangler families no doubt reclaimed their wood to its peacetime purpose – domestic use. Not surprisingly, the remaining defenses fell into low nondescript mounds. In 1873, in his early guidebook to the field, John Bachelder noted, "It is to be regretted, however, that greater efforts have not been made to preserve [the defenses]; and even now they could easily be rebuilt, and would make lasting monuments for the study of future generations." In the summer of 1881, improvements were initiated by the Gettysburg Battlefield Memorial Association, including stone and dirt reconstructions of the defenses along their original lines, and sodding the work to prevent erosion. 1.

Evidently omitted from the early reconstruction, little evidence remains of Colgrove's defenses in McAllister's Woods. Appearing on the 1869 Warren Survey Map, these breastworks appeared in field reports for the Park as late as

1943, where the remaining section is described as being fifty yards in length, but that parts were "nearly level with the adjoining terrain." Although the site was recommended for improvement, it appears little, if anything, was done to restore this area. 2

Also gone from Culp's Hill is any evidence of the traverse that became so invaluable in the defense of the upper summit (see Footnotes for July 2). The location of the breastworks seems clear–both Brig. Gen. Greene and the 1869 Warren Survey Map locate them perpendicular to the angle in the main breastworks north of the saddle. In Peter Rothermel's detailed painting of Steuart's charge on July 3, a log breastwork appears on the site, and connects with the "shelf of rocks" occupied by Kane's brigade. If Rothermel's depiction is correct, this wood was no doubt reclaimed after the battle as well. Perhaps unaware of the importance of the site, the GBMA eventually removed any remaining sections around 1887 during breastwork reconstruction. Whatever the reason, it is unfortunate no trace remains of this significant piece of the struggle for Culp's Hill. 3

Early view of McAllister's Dam on Rock Creek.

130

Rock Creek

Although not evident today, in 1863 Rock Creek, and particularly the mill pond above McAllister's Dam, presented a formidable obstacle to any Southern movement around the Federal right. In his report of the battle, Brig. Gen. Colgrove describes the water there as, "some 60 to 80 feet in width and from 6 to 8 feet deep rendering the position...unassailable from the east or south." With the collapse of McAllister's dam in 1877, the profile of Rock Creek changed significantly. Calling for the Battlefield Commissioners to restore the dam, a local newspaper article described:

> In those days before the bursting of McAllister's Dam, the dammed waters of Rock Creek reached beyond the State Road [Route 30]. The Creek most of the year was a pretentious stream bank full. There was a time when boys...could get a very decent journey by poling up or down the creek.

The dam was eventually repaired, but again in 1878 the barrier, "was finally swept away, and made the creek the wreck of today, instead of a fine body of water." 4

Early Avenues

One of the most significant alterations to Culp's Hill was the construction of avenues to provide access to the area. Ironically, in doing so, the greatest damage to the site may not have resulted from an influx of visitors, but by those seeking to commemorate the area.

Previous to the 1880's, those visiting Culp's Hill traveled the same unimproved lanes extant in 1863. Finally, in July of 1881 the Gettysburg Battlefield Memorial Association began work on what became known as Slocum Avenue, connecting Cemetery Hill with Spangler's Spring. After the establishment of the Gettysburg National Military Park

Photo looks south across the 1890's path of Slocum Avenue on the upper summit. The 66th Ohio monument is at left of view. (1897 GNMP Reports)

Commission, Slocum Avenue was improved in 1896 with the "Telford" process - grading the roadbed and adding layers of crushed stone. However, in view of Commission reports that indicated, "particular care is also taken to avoid cutting away and changing the natural surface of the ground when constructing the avenues," the path chosen for Slocum Avenue was unfortunate. Following the early trail from Stevens Knoll, the avenue paralleled the First Corps' works on the north side of the hill, and then crisscrossed Greene's defenses on the steep eastern slope, before winding around the southern side of the crest to the present course of Slocum Avenue (see accompanying map). Even with the retaining walls visible in photographs, the sheer slope undoubtedly made for a dramatic, but harrowing, carriage ride; sadly, it also permanently altered the fragile face of the upper summit. 5

By 1899, the path that became Geary Avenue was also improved with the Telford process. Here, one of the costs was evidently part of Spangler's Spring. In early postwar photographs, the site appears as two separate rock-walled springs: one appears to be at the modern site, the other about 10 yards beyond and to the northeast (see photo accompanying STOP 2). By 1900, photographs indicate the northern spring and the surrounding stack of boulders had disappeared under the path of the new Geary Avenue. The disappearance of historic rock formations elsewhere on the hill, as well as evidence of substantial quarrying, indicate the convenience of nearby materials was taking precedence over preservation concerns. 6

To the Commission's credit, other (hopefully) less destructive improvements soon followed: the marking of Confederate positions was finally initiated, and with the purchase of 41 acres from the Culp family, East Confederate Avenue was laid out. The 1900's would see the construction of Williams, Colgrove, and Carman Avenues. The northern sections of Slocum Avenue would eventually be rerouted; although attempts were made to restore the site by removing the roadbed, there is evidence today of substantial erosion where the path crossed the eastern face. 7

Circa 1899 view of the Telford process on Geary Avenue (1899 GNMP Reports)

Turn-of-the-century path of Slocum Avenue behind the 150th New York monument. (1897 GNMP Reports)

Modern photo of original Slocum Avenue trace. The current path of Slocum Avenue crosses the middle of the view.

NOTES

Introduction

1. John Bachelder, *Gettysburg: What to See How to See It,* (Boston: J.B. Bachelder, 1873), 93; Harlan D. Unrau *Administrative History of Gettysburg National Military Park and Cemetery,* (United States Dept. of Interior/National Park Service, July 1991), 5.

July 1

1. Edwin B. Coddington, *The Gettysburg Campaign – A Study In Command,* (New York, Scribner's Sons, 1968), 237, 266, 310-1; David L. & Audrey J. Ladd, Ed. *The Bachelder Papers - Gettysburg in Their Own Words,* 3 vols. (New Hampshire Historical Society, 1994, Printed by Morningside Press, Dayton, Ohio) (Hereafter referred to as *B.P.*) Letter of Capt. C. Horton, 1/23/67, Vol. 1, 290. The explosions from modern fireworks displays near Oak Ridge in Gettysburg can easily be heard today at Two Taverns. Due to the possibility of an acoustic "shadow" created by other terrain or weather conditions, we can not know how much of the morning's battle could be heard during Slocum's march or after their arrival at Two Taverns. In any event, there would have been little noise around noon when a lull occurred in the fighting.

3. *The Gettysburg Campaign,* 237, 266-7; U.S. War Department, *The War of the Rebellion: A Compilation of the Official Records of the Union and Confederate Armies,* 70 vols. in 128 parts (Washington, D.C.: Government Printing Office, 1880-1901), Series 1, Vol. 27, Part 1, 701-702. (Hereinafter referred to as *O.R..* Unless noted, all references are from Series 1, Vol. 27).

4. Ibid., Part 3, pp. 457-8, 463-4.

5. *The Gettysburg Campaign,* 310-1; *O.R.* Part 1, 126. Slocum's movements that morning, and possibly his odd hesitation afterward, may have been caused by directions contained in the "Pipe Creek Circular," a supplemental dispatch from the Army's new commander, Maj. Gen. George G. Meade. The provisionary order described a defensive line near Westminster in Maryland to be taken up should the Army of the Potomac be unable to fight the enemy on their own terms. The fall-back position lay down the

Baltimore Pike, about twelve miles south of Slocum's position at Two Taverns.

6. *O.R.*, Part 2, 484; John Busey & David Martin *Regimental Strengths and Losses at Gettysburg* (Hightstown, N.J.: Longstreet House, 1986), 286 (Unless noted, all regimental strengths and losses are from this title); Report of Lt. Col. C. Morgan, *B.P.* (3), 1350. Brig. Gen. R.F. Hoke was recovering from wounds received at Chancellorsville two months before. The last regiment of the brigade, the 54th North Carolina, was on detached duty and did not rejoin the brigade until after the battle.

7. *O.R.*, Part 1, 366, 704.

8. Charles Hamlin, et al *Maine at Gettysburg* (Portland: Lakeside Press, 1898), 89: *O.R.*, Part 2, 484.

9. *O.R.*, Part 1, 757-8. According to Hancock's chief of staff, Lt. Col. Charles Morgan, Slocum arrived and took over command between 5:00 and 6:00 p.m. See *B.P.* (3), 1352.

10. *O.R.*, Part 1, 366; Kenneth Bandy & Florence Freeland *The Gettysburg Papers* Vol. 1 (Dayton, Ohio: Morningside Press, 1978), Account of Rufus Dawes, 383-4.

11. *O.R.*, Part 2, 445; Harry W. Pfanz *Gettysburg - Culp's Hill and Cemetery Hill* (Chapel Hill, Univ. of N.C .Press, 1993), 73-78.

12. *O.R.*, Part 2, 446, 469-70. *Gettysburg - Culp's Hill and Cemetery Hill*, 80. Lee would meet with Ewell, Early and Rodes on the evening of July 1 to discuss Ewell's extended position in front of Cemetery and Culp's Hills. It was Lee's impression, initially at least, that the extended line should be pulled back to Seminary Ridge with Hill's Corps. He later deferred when Ewell suggested seizing Culp's Hill. See Coddington, 365-7.

13. *O.R.*, Part 2, 504, 526, 531, 537; John Goldsborough White, "A 'Rebel's' Recollections" *The Sun* (Baltimore) May, 19, 1929, copy in 2nd Maryland vertical file, GNMP; Newspaper account of "S.Z.A." from the Baltimore *Telegram*, p. 131. From a clipping scrapbook of the 1879 series by members of the 2nd Maryland, copy in 2nd Maryland vertical file, GNMP. The content and style of these writings indicate "S.Z.A." drew heavily from the accounts of Maj. William Goldsborough.

14. O.R., Part 1, p. 284-5; Regimental Strengths and Losses, 24.

15. *O.R.*, Part 1, p. 284-5; *O.R.*, Part 2, 446; Orville Thomson, *Narrative of Service of the 7th Indiana*, (no pub., no date), copy in 7th

Indiana vertical file, GNMP. The 7th was on detached guard duty in Emmitsburg, Maryland, and missed the first day's fighting
16. *O.R.*, Part 2, 446

July 2: Morning

1. The Gettysburg Campaign, 333-7. Gettysburg - Culp's Hill and Cemetery Hill, 117.
2. *O.R.*, Part 1, 759, 825. As understood by Slocum, the arrangement now placed him in command of the right "wing" at Gettysburg, and he designated Brig. Gen. Alpheus Williams to command the Twelfth Corps in his stead.
3. *Regimental Strengths and Losses*, 256; *O.R.*, Part 1, 765-70, 855-6. New York Monuments commission for the Battlefields at Gettysburg and Chattanooga, *Final Report of the Battlefield of Gettysburg*, 3 Vols. (Albany: J.B. Lyon Co., 1902) (Hereinafter known as *N.Y. at Gettysburg*) Vol. 2, 1011; Robert Johnson and Clarence Buel *Battles and Leaders of the Civil War* (Hereinafter known as *B&L*) Vol. 3 (New York: Century Co. 1884-9) 316 .
4. *O.R.*, Part 1, 836, 847-57; Letter of Capt. C. Horton, 1/23/67, *B.P.* (1), 291; Letter of Lt. Col. J. Mitchell, 66th Ohio, 8/15/87, *B.P.* (3), 1507; Letter of Capt. William Alexander, 111th New York, 9/2/87, *B.P.* (3), 1510-11; *Regimental Strengths and Losses*, 256. Although Capt. Alexander of Geary's staff suggests the 66th Ohio began construction of this line of works, and Capt. Horton claimed Greene's men started "the first tracings of this work," there is no definite record of which unit constructed these works. As Mitchell and others in Candy's brigade also mention building defenses, it seems just as likely they had a hand in their construction. It is just as possible that a competent engineer such as Greene called for such a defense to be built. After Kane's line extended to the lower hill, the perpendicular line of unused works technically became a "traverse." See Appendix.
5. *Regimental Strengths and Losses*, 255. *O.R.*, Part 1, 788-803, 812;. In his report, Colgrove claimed that Ruger later ordered him to shift the 13th New Jersey and the 107th New York to McAllister's woods, and to place his smallest regiment, the 3rd Wisconsin on McDougall's right. Although it seems logical, no one else reported as such. As the second position is similar to that of July 3, perhaps Colgrove confused them.

6. *O.R.*, Part 1, 766, 804; Letter of Brig. Gen. A. Williams, 4/7/64, *B.P.* (1), 146.

7. *O.R.*, Part 1, 826, 836, 845, 856, 862; Diary of Lt. Robert Cruickshank, p. 122-3, Original manuscript at Bancroft Public Library, Salem, NY, copy on file GNMP.

8. The Gettysburg Campaign, 337-8.

9. *O.R.*, Part 2, 504,531, 518; *Regimental Strengths and Losses*, 285; Capt. George Thomas, Excerpt of Dedication of 2nd Maryland monument, 11/19/1886, copy in 2nd Maryland vertical file, GNMP. Thomas was with Company A of Steuart's 2nd Maryland.

10. *O.R.*, Part 2, 446; Account of "S.Z.A.," Baltimore *Telegram,* 131. Although no written evidence has surfaced, there appears to be evidence that defenses were erected on the Lady farm.

11. Randolph H. McKim *A Soldier's Recollections* (New York: Longmans, Green & Co., 1910) 184, 194-5. McKim was Brig. Gen. Steuart's aide-de-camp during the campaign. With the advantage of hindsight, McKim's analysis of the battle places blame with Lee's subordinates for the loss at Gettysburg; Account of "S.Z.A.," Baltimore *Telegram,* 131.

12. William W. Goldsborough *The Maryland Line In the Confederate States Army* (Baltimore: Kelly, Piet & Co. 1869), 141-2 (hereafter known as *Maryland Line*, 1869). Goldsborough published two versions of this work, one in 1869, another revised edition in 1900; several discrepancies appear between the two.

13. *O.R.*, Part 2, 446-7; Jay Jorgensen "Joseph W. Latimer, the 'Boy Major' at Gettysburg" *Gettysburg Magazine*, (January, 1994), 30-1. Of the eighty-odd guns available to him, Ewell decided to use only thirty-two pieces to shell the Federal position. In addition to Latimer's guns, three batteries of Dance's Battalion were in position by the Seminary buildings behind Ewell's right.

July 2: Afternoon

1. John Nicholson, ed. Pennsylvania at Gettysburg: Ceremonies at the Dedication of the Monuments Erected by the Commonwealth of Pennsylvania 2 vols. (Harrisburg: W. Stanley Ray, State Printer, 1904), 881; Edward Marcus, ed. A New Canaan Private in the Civil War; The Letters of Justus M. Silliman (New Canaan, CT: New Canaan Historical Society, 1884), 42.

2. *O.R.*, Part 1, 826, 860, 863. In the eyes of those on Culp's Hill, it was their fire that eventually silenced the Confederate artillery.

3. *O.R.*, Part 2, 531, 536, 539.

4. *Maine at Gettysburg*, p. 93; L. Van Loan Naisawald *Grape and Canister* (New York: Oxford Univ. Press, 1960) p. 402; *O.R.*, Part 2, 543-4.

5. *O.R.*, Part 1, 862; Part 2, 531, 536.

6. *Gettysburg - Culp's Hill and Cemetery Hill*, 187; Text of Latimer's Monuments, Benner's Hill, GNMP; *O.R.*, Part 2, 543-4.

7. *O.R.*, Part 2, 556.

8. *O.R.*, Part 2, 504, 532, 537; White, "A 'Rebel's' Recollections"; "S.Z.A." account, Baltimore *Telegram*, p. 132.

9. *O.R.*, Part 2, 504, 509, 513, 532; White, "A 'Rebel's' Recollections"; "S.Z.A." account, Baltimore *Telegram*, p. 132; "On the Right at Gettysburg," Account of Sgt. Martin Olmsted (Co. H, 102nd N.Y.), *National Tribune* (December 17, 1908), 5. The command of Nicholls' brigade fell to Col. Williams after Brig. Gen. Nicholls was wounded at Chancellorsville. The final arrangement Johnson's division would take during the advance is unclear.

10. *O.R.*, Part 2, 504, 518.

11. *O.R.*, Part 2, 509, 513, 518; Walter Clark, ed. *Histories of the Several Regiments and Battalions From North Carolina in the Great War, 1861-1865* 5 vols. (Raleigh: State of North Carolina, 1901), Vol. 1, 195 (Hereafter referred to as *North Carolina in the War*). The 1st Maryland Battalion was later officially designated the 2nd Maryland Regiment. The unit was known as the 1st Maryland during the battle and is designated as such in this study. The early Battlefield Commission preferred the later title to avoid confusion with Federal Maryland units. Close examination of their monument reveals the veterans still had their way. The order for Steuart's advance is from Goldsborough's 1900 edition of *The Maryland Line In the Confederate Army*. Another account places the 23rd Virginia on the left, followed by the 37th and 10th Virginia, then the 1st Maryland and 3rd North Carolina on the right (see "S.Z.A." account, Baltimore *Telegram*, 132). In his memoirs, the adjutant of the 23rd Virginia, Charles A. Raine, also places his regiment on the left of the advance; perhaps the 10th Virginia ended up behind the 23rd Virginia during the advance. There is

no way to reconcile the difference, but Goldsborough's order seems correct considering later events.

12. Letter of Lt. Charles B. Brockway to David McConaughy, 3/5/64, General Correspondence file, Peter Rothermel Papers, Pennsylvania Historical Collection, State Archives; *O.R.*, Part 1, 894; *O.R.* 2, 536-9. In 1863, those on Cemetery Hill had a good view of Benner's Hill at least as far south as the Benner farm before Culp's Hill obscured the southern slope. Today, the woods northeast of Culp's Hill obscure much of the vista.

July 2: Evening

1. *O.R.*, Part 1, 862.

2. Journal of John H. Stone, Co. B, copy in 2nd Maryland vertical file, GNMP. Several accounts from Johnson's division described Redington's skirmishers as a line of battle.

3. *O.R.*, Part 2, 532.

4 "On the Right At Gettysburg," *National Tribune* (December 17, 1908), p. 5.

5. "S.Z.A." account, Baltimore *Telegram*, 132. ;*The Maryland Line*, 1869, 146.

6. *O.R.*, Part 2, 510

7. *O.R.*, Part 1, 862.

8. *O.R.*, Part 2, 510; *The Maryland Line*, 1869, 148.

9. Letter of Brig. Gen. A. Williams, 11/10/65, *B.P.* (1), 215; *Gettysburg - Culp's Hill and Cemetery Hill*, 194. No record survives of Maj. Gen. Meade's exact orders to Slocum. Whether Meade ordered the entire Twelfth Corps to abandon Culp's Hill as Slocum later claimed, or "all the troops he could spare," as Brig. Gen. Williams wrote, Slocum's initial response was to send Williams with a division. Reports place the time of the move by the First Division anywhere from 4:00 to 6:30 p.m.. Judging by other events on the field, about 5:30 or 6:00 p.m. seems likely.

10. Gettysburg - Culp's Hill and Cemetery Hill, 194; O.R., Part 1, 826; Charles C. Fennell, Jr., Attack and Defense of Culp's Hill: Greene's Brigade at the Battle of Gettysburg (Hanover, PA : Doctoral thesis - West Virginia University, 1992) Dr. Fennell, a Licensed Battlefield Guide at Gettysburg, suggests that the withdrawal of the Twelfth Corps skirmish line was reported to Ewell, prompting his decision to attack.

11. *N.Y. at Gettysburg* (2) 942; *O.R.*, Part 1, 856, 866. Brig. Gen. Greene did not specify how this move was accomplished. Statements by Greene, Ireland, and others seem to indicate that Ireland's large regiment was shifted en masse and at the double quick, placing their left on the north side of the saddle where the regiment's right stood initially; this would allow each unit to file right independently. The second position of the 137th New York is not marked today, but allowing for those on skirmish duty, Ireland's 423-man regiment would have easily reached the far side of the lower hill. Spangler's Wall crosses the breastworks there about 340 yards from the north side of the saddle and would have been a convenient anchor for Ireland's right. See also *O.R.*, Part 1, 862, 864; *B&L*, III, 316; *N.Y. at Gettysburg* (2) 1013; Sergeant Henry Rudy Diary, transcript in 137th New York vertical file, GNMP.

12. *O.R.*, Part 1, 860, 863-4 866. *N.Y. at Gettysburg* (2) 1012-3; Capt. George Collins, *Memoirs of the 149th New York Volunteer Infantry*, (Syracuse, G.K. Collins: 1891, reprint by Edmonston Publishing Inc., 1995) 138. Depending on the arrival of First Corps reinforcements, it is possible the 60th New York temporarily stretched to their left to cover the former position of the 78th New York.

13. *B&L*, III, 316.

14. *Ibid.*; *O.R.*, Part 1, 862; Letter of Capt. Steuben Coon, transcript in 60th New York vertical file, GNMP.

July 2: Night

1. *O.R.*, Part 2, 538; Account of Benj. Anderson Jones, CWTI Collection, USAMHI, copy in 44th Virginia vertical file, GNMP.

2. *O.R.*, Part 2, 531; Letter of Capt. C.R. Skinker, Original in Brock Collection, copy in 48th Virginia vertical file, GNMP. Accounts of both Jones' and Nicholls' brigade mention at least three separate charges. Brig. Gen. Greene mentions "four distinct charges between 7 and 9:30 p.m." It is possible the charges by Johnson's brigades were coordinated, but conditions on the hillside make this unlikely.

3. Letter of Capt. Steuben Coon; Account of Benj. Anderson Jones, CWTI collection U.S.A.M.H.I., copy in 44th VA vertical file, GNMP.

4. *O.R.*, Part 2, 531, 533.

5. *O.R.*, Part 2, 513; Account of Capt. Nathan Rawling, copy in 14th LA vertical file, GNMP; Account of W.P. Snakenberg, 14th LA vertical file, GNMP. In the confusion, the Southern color bearer tore the regimental flag from its staff, and hid it beneath his jacket. He kept the prize concealed during his imprisonment, and returned it to the regiment following his exchange.

6. Goldsborough, *Maryland Line*, (1900),103-4; Account of "S.Z.A.," Baltimore *Telegram*, 132.

7. Randolph H. McKim, *A Soldier's Recollections* (New York: Longmans, Green & Co., 1910) 195-6. One has to wonder where Lt. Col. H.A. Brown, commanding the 1st North Carolina, was during this episode.

8. Goldsborough, *Maryland Line*, 1869, 149; Account of "S.Z.A.," Baltimore *Telegram*, 133. Perhaps Steuart's oblique movement had overlapped the brigade lines, for Walton's 23rd Virginia should have been two regiments to the left.

9. *O.R.*, Part 1, 866.

10. Memoir of Charles A. Raines, copy in 23rd Virginia vertical file, GNMP; Goldsborough, *Maryland Line*, (1900), 104.

11. *The Windsor (N.Y.) Standard*, June 29, 1894, copy in 137th New York vertical file, GNMP; *O.R.*, Part 2, 510.

12. *O.R.*, Part 1, 856-7; *N.Y. at Gettysburg* (2), 1002. Most of the First Corps units lost heavily during the first day's fighting - the 6th Wisconsin, and 84th and 147th New York totaled less than 375 men. Little is known about the role of the 76th and 95th New York, but their markers place them on the crest between the 7th Indiana and 60th New York. *O.R.*, Part 1, 735, 738. Greene also reported that the 61st Ohio, 82nd Illinois, and the 45th and 157th New York of the Eleventh Corps relieved his men in the trenches; again, it is unclear what role they took in the defense of the hill. The terse reports for the 61st Ohio and 157th New York indicate they occupied the wall on the lower hill but were driven off. See also *Gettysburg - Culp's Hill and Cemetery Hill*, 213-4.

13. *O.R.*, Part 1, 856, 866; Letter of R.P. Smith, July 29, 1863, copy in 71st Pennsylvania vertical file, GNMP. There is some question as to the position occupied by the 71st Pennsylvania. If they replaced the right company of the 137th as Ireland stated, it seems to indicate they also took up a refused position. The road mentioned

by Smith is probably Spangler's Lane, which remains as a trace to the northwest.

14. *O.R.* Part 1, 277; Letter of Lt. Col. R. Dawes, 3/18/68, *B.P.* (1), 327. Neither of the First Corps regiments mention seeing the 137th New York, so it is possible these units arrived shortly before, or concurrent with Ireland's withdrawal. It is unlikely we will ever know the sequence of the desperate fighting in this area, but this seems a likely scenario.

15. Letter of Col. E.B. Fowler, 10/2/89, *B.P.* (3), 1638.

16. *O.R.*, Part 1, 866; B&L, 317.

17. *O.R.*, Part 1, 866; *O.R.*, Part 2, 510.

18. Account of "S.Z.A.," Baltimore *Telegram*, 132; *O.R.*, Part 2, 510.

19. O.R. Part 2, 513, 537; Paper of Col. David Zable, 14th Louisiana, original in Howard-Tilton Memorial Library, Tulane Univ., copy on file in Nicholls' Brigade vertical file, GNMP. Located on East Confederate Avenue below the upper summit, early Battlefield Commission records describe this wall as "Jones' Breastworks," and the marker for Jones' brigade is located here.

20. Goldsborough, *Maryland Line* (1900), 104; *Maryland Line* (1869), 152; *O.R.*, Part 2, 510. According to Goldsborough, because Johnson was, "not a Stonewall Jackson" he allowed the opportunity to pass. A belief that the Federals were retreating was expressed in Goldsborough's 1869 version of *The Maryland Line*. The scouting story appears in the 1900 version of this work; it seems odd that Goldsborough neglected to include the latter story in his 1869 version.

July 2 - July 3

1. *O.R.*, Part 1, 759-60, 851.

2. *O.R.*, Part 1, 849-53, 855; Moses Veale, *The 109th Regiment Penna. Veteran Volunteers*, (Philadelphia, n.p., 1890) 14; *Pennsylvania at Gettysburg* (1), 220; Letter of Capt. W. Alexander, 111th Pennsylvania, 9/2/87, *B.P.* (3) 1511. The 29th Pennsylvania had 357 men at Gettysburg, somewhat more than the 109th and 111th put together. According to Greene, a staff officer was sent to lead Kane's men back safely back to his flank. If so, why he did not recommend a more sensible position is a mystery.

3. *O.R.*, Part 1, 351; *O.R.*, Part 1, 849-53, 855. For more on the traverse see Appendix. Ill at the start of the campaign, Brig. Gen.

Kane returned to his brigade at Gettysburg, but was still too weak and again turned command over to Cobham. Both Kane and Cobham submitted reports for the brigade, but indicate orders were given by Cobham. Oddly, neither Kane nor Cobham described the initial position in the saddle.

4. *O.R.*, Part 1, 827, 837, 839, 840, 846 *Pennsylvania at Gettysburg*, 717. Lt. Col. Ario Pardee was the only one to report that the line actually had this configuration.

5. *O.R.*, Part 1, 775, 780. There would be several claims to early accidental encounters with Johnson's men, particularly at Spangler's Spring. Not surprisingly, legend grew afterward that a truce of sorts existed while the exhausted opponents shared the springs that night; the sources for the story are less clear. The first widely published account appears in *Pennsylvania at Gettysburg*, and mentions a member of McDougall's 46th Pennsylvania going to fill canteens and, finding Rebels at the spring, "he backed out with the best grace he could command." Not published until 1929, the diary of Cpl. Horatio Chapman of the 20th Connecticut also describes finding, "quite a large number at the spring and it was so dark...and although all was still and not a word spoken, yet we well knew that they were Rebels and they also knew that the Yanks were there." Although both sides may have drawn water at same time, one has to wonder if the fury of the recent battle would not preclude any fraternization. *Pennsylvania at Gettysburg* (1), 308; Diary of Horatio Chapman, 7/2/1863, Original in Connecticut State Library, copy on file GNMP Library.

6. *O.R.*, Part 1, 780, 811, 815, 817. In a speech in 1878, Morse indicated only his skirmishers advanced north of the swale. His original report and that of the 107th New York indicate otherwise. McAllister's Woods must have been getting crowded, for after their return, the New York regiment formed in column behind McDougall's brigade.

7. *O.R.*, Part 1, 780, 783, 790-1, 798 The exact arrangement of McDougall's regiments is unclear. It seems possible the 20th Connecticut formed the left of the brigade at this point.

8. *O.R.*, Part 1, 780

9. Letter of Brig. Gen. A. Williams, 11/10/65, *B.P.* (1), 219-220; *O.R.*, Part 1, 775, 761.

10. *O.R.* Part 2, 320.

July 3: Morning

1. *O.R.* Part 2, 447.

2. Ibid.

3. *The Gettysburg Campaign – A Study In Command*, 454; *O.R.* part 2, 521, 568, 593. With the exception of the 2nd Virginia, Walker's brigade was moved to support Steuart while Smith's men took over the position at the meadow.

4. *O.R.*, Part 1, 775, McKim, 199.

5. *O.R.*, Part 1, 775, 820, 871. The other guns involved were Rigby's Battery A, 1st Maryland Artillery, Rugg's Battery E, 4th U.S., and Kinzie's Battery K, 5th U.S. Artillery.

6. O.R., Part 1, 804, 806, 820; In the report for the 2nd Virginia, Nadenbousch describes advancing a flanking party to "a bend of the creek, some 60 yards to the rear and left," to repel an attack; he could be describing this advance by Lockwood or Colgrove's later advance. See *O.R.* part 2, 521. Col. Crane of the 107th New York describes the attack as lasting 20 minutes before the regiment retired "in some disorder." The monuments for the 1st Md. P.H.B. place the regiment facing east with their left at the wall on the lower slope, and their right south of Spangler's Spring, which if accurately marked, seems an unlikely spot to endanger another Federal regiment.

7. *O.R.*, Part 1, 780, 784, 793. Eventually, the regiment held a line so far up the hillside that several of the Connecticut men also would fall victim to their own artillery.

8. *O.R.*, Part 1, 781; Letter of Brig. Gen. T. Ruger, 8/12/69, *B.P.* (1), 363-4. The times given for the action vary from 5:00 a.m. to 10:00 a.m. There appears to be no way to reconcile the difference. Reports for the regiments involved claim the earlier times, which also seem to make more sense.

9. *O.R.*, Part 1, 813. One might wonder if Slocum, in skipping Williams in the chain of command, did not also send an aide to Colgrove with the initial order.

10. Charles F. Morse, History of the Second Massachusetts Regiment at Gettysburg (Boston, George Ellis, 1882), 13-4.

11. *O.R.*, Part 1, 813-5; *B.P.* (3), 1772-3. Edmund R. Brown, *The Twenty-seventh Indiana in the War of the Rebellion*, (n.p., 1899), 380-3. Johnson describes this attack as being met by the 2nd Virginia and

Smith's brigade; the 1st North Carolina may have been ordered to the western slope by this point. In 1890 letters to John Bachelder proposing this marker, the inscription was to be, "eleven color bearers were successively shot down at this point..." Bachelder probably directed the inscription to say what it reads today.

12. *O.R.*, Part 2, 521; *History of the Second Massachusetts*, 14-5; *The Gettysburg Papers*, Vol. 2, 833. The report for Smith's brigade briefly describes an advance by the 49th and 52nd Virginia to drive a Yankee attack from Steuart's flank.

13. Pennsylvania at Gettysburg, (2), 717.

14. *O.R.*, Part 1, 839, 840-1, 846; *Pennsylvania at Gettysburg*, (2), 718. Both Ohio regiments mention a stone wall in the area: the 5th Ohio mentions one on their flank used for shelter, and the 7th Ohio describes a wall "which runs parallel with the road leading to the pike." Warren's survey map of the area indicates a wood fence bordering Spangler's Lane; these accounts may indicate that at least part of the fence straddled a stone wall. Just after sunrise, the 7th Ohio was withdrawn from the right of the Pennsylvania line, and moved to the hollow to support Greene's brigade.

15. *O.R.*, Part 1, 829, 849, 856-7. Greene states the First and Eleventh Corps regiments returned to their commands at this point. Lockwood's last regiment, the 1st Maryland Eastern Shore, arrived at about 8:00 a.m. on July 3.

16. *Memoirs of the 149th New York*, 140-1. All of Geary's front line appears to have been relieved except for Candy's regiments in front of Spangler's Lane.

17. Ibid., 144, 149-50. The relief on the monument for the 149th New York depicts the color-bearer, William Lilly, mending the flag.

18. Letter of Brig. Gen. A. Williams, 11/10/65, *B.P.* (1), 221

19. *O.R.*, Part 2, 593.

20. *O.R.*, Part 2, 505, 536, 568-9. "Paper Read by Col. David Zable at Meeting of Army of Northern Virginia, Louisiana Division, December 12, 1903," 3, Manuscript copy, Nicholls' Brigade vertical file, GNMP (Original in Howard-Tilton Memorial Library, Tulane Univ.). In his report, Johnson describes three separate attacks. From the perspective of those on the front line, the fighting was continuous.

21. *O.R.*, Part 2, 504, 511, 519; Account of "S.Z.A.," Baltimore *Telegram,* 135; Account of W.W. Goldsborough, newspaper clipping from Brake Collection, Box 7, USAMHI, copy on file 2nd Maryland vertical file, GNMP.

22. *A Soldier's Recollections,* 184-5 Although Goldsborough indicates some of his companies were relieved, McKim claimed Steuart's men had no support whatsoever.

23. *O.R.*, Part 2, 504, 568, 593, 601. From Louis Leon, *Diary of a Tar Heel Confederate Soldier* (Charlotte, NC: 1913, Stone Publishing) 36-7; "Zable Paper," 3. Leon was a private in the 53rd North Carolina; a copy of his diary edited by Gregory Mast can be found on the Gettysburg Discussion Group Website. It is unclear whether Walker's and Daniels' regiments supported Steuart's line or relieved them. O'Neal's accounts also provide few clear details of how his attack was made.

24. O.R., Part 2, 447; A Soldier's Recollections, 205.

25. *O.R.*, Part 2, 511; *The Maryland Line* (1900 Edition), 106

26. *O.R.*, Part 2, 511; Account of D. Ridgely Howard, "Left on the Field", *Baltimore Telegram,* 139; *The Maryland Line* (1900 Edition), 109.

27. *A Soldier's Recollections,* 205. In a footnote to his text, McKim quotes this passage but does not identify the writer. Account of D. Ridgely Howard, "Left on the Field," *Baltimore Telegram,* 139. Ironically, part of Lockwood's 1st Maryland E.S. may have been the "second line" referred to (see *O.R.*, Part 1, 804); badly wounded minutes later, D. R. Howard was pulled inside Union lines. After identifying his unit, his captors asked, "Do you know you are fighting your own men?" Howard replied, "Yes, and we intend to fight them."

28. Account of General Thomas Kane, 3/28/74, Rothermel Papers, PA Historical and Museum Collection.

29. *Pennsylvania at Gettysburg* (1), 220 Apparently, the failure to advance by the left of the line created the appearance as "advancing by battalion." It appears Daniels' 43rd and 53rd North Carolina began to move in support of Steuart, but the attack failed before they advanced far.

30. Account of "S.Z.A.," Baltimore Telegram, 136; A Soldier's Recollections, 204-5.

31. Account of General Thomas Kane, 3/28/74, Rothermel papers. The episode was included in Rothermel's painting of the charge. Although it is possible the animal was a mascot, it seems odd there is no mention in 1st Maryland accounts.

32. *O.R.*, Part 2, 527, 592-3; S. R. Norris, "Ohio at Gettysburg" *National Tribune,* June 9, 1887, copy on file GNMP library. Although there are several vivid accounts by members of the 7th Ohio, unfortunately we can only guess where they fought. The monument for the regiment indicates a support position on the right of Greene's brigade, probably to keep it near Candy's brigade line. The report of the regiment describes briefly relieving the 60th New York, falling back and then relieving "some other regiment," from 9:30 a.m. until that evening; it seems likely that their position was near Greene's left center.

33. Account of Sgt. Lawrence Wilson, (Co. D., 7th Ohio) *Washington Post,* July 9, 1899, copy on file GNMP library; Olmsted Account, *National Tribune* (December 17, 1908), 5; *O.R.*, Part 2, 519.

July 3: Afternoon

1. *O.R.*, Part 2, 505; Account of "S.Z.A.," Baltimore *Telegram,* 137.

2. *O.R.*, Part 1, 784-5, 794; Cruickshank Manuscript, 127.

3. Account of "S.Z.A.," Baltimore *Telegram,* 137. *O.R.*, Part 1, 785, 794; Brown, *The Twenty-seventh Indiana in the War of the Rebellion,* 386. Kane's brigade formed on McDougall's left soon after, reoccupying their original line of defenses in the saddle and lower summit.

4. Sgt. Henry Morhous, *Reminiscences of the 123rd Regiment, N.Y.S.V.* (Greenwich, N.Y., People's Journal Book Office, 1879), 50-1. *Memoirs of the 149th New York Volunteer Infantry,* 146. Although unnerving, the extreme range of these rounds probably caused few casualties.

5. Account of "S.Z.A.," Baltimore Telegram, 137; Memoirs of the 149th New York Volunteer Infantry, 147

Aftermath

1. *Memoirs of the 149th New York Volunteer Infantry,* 147-8; Letter of Sgt. Sam Lusk, July 7, 1863, 137th New York Vertical File, GNMP library

2. H.E. Brown, The 28th Regiment P.V.V.I., the 147th Regiment. P.V.V.I., and Knap's Independent Battery E at Gettysburg (no publisher., no date) 7, pages on file, GNMP library; Memoirs of the 149th New York Volunteer Infantry, 147-8. Letter of Sgt. L.R. Coy, copy on file, 123rd NY Vertical file GNMP

3. S. R. Norris, "Ohio at Gettysburg" *National Tribune,* June 9, 1887, copy on file GNMP library. It appears there was not time to bury all the Southern dead. Norris' letter was written in response to the initial omission of 7th Ohio from a report by the Ohio Monument Commission. He also wrote, no doubt bitterly: "If the death list of these regiments at that engagement was not large enough to be commemorated in marble with their comrades from the more unfortunate organizations, erect the monuments to commemorate the services the living rendered their country."

4. *Regimental Strengths and Losses,* 285-7. Even among the survivors, there were conflicting figures for Southern losses on Culp's Hill. Busey and Martin's study appears to be the most consistent. Johnson's casualties are listed as 381 killed, 1168 wounded, 453 missing or captured (2,002 out of 6,433), or almost one-third of those engaged. The figures for Rodes two brigades under Daniels and O'Neal can only be guessed due to heavy casualties on July 1. An estimate would say the two brigades probably reached Culp's Hill with about 2,475 men; a conservative estimate of their losses would be 375, or 15%. Smith's Brigade of Early's Division lost 213 of 806 (46-115-52), or 26% of those engaged on Culp's Hill.

5. *Regimental Strengths and Losses,* 255-7. While the entire Twelfth Corps suffered 10% casualties of its number, the 137th New York and 27th Indiana each lost 32%, and the 2nd Massachusetts lost 43% of those engaged.

6. Memoirs of the 149th New York Volunteer Infantry, 150.

Appendix

1. John Bachelder, *Gettysburg: What to See How to See It,* (Boston: J.B. Bachelder, 1873), 93; Harlan D. Unrau *Administrative History of Gettysburg National Military Park and Cemetery,* (United States Dept. of Interior/National Park Service, July 1991), 49.

2. National Park Service, *Field Defenses on the Battlefield at Gettysburg,* Report cover letter dated 4/20/43; copy on file GNMP library.

3. *O.R.,* Part 1, 836, 847-57; Letter of Capt. C. Horton, 1/23/67, *B.P.* (1), 291; Letter of Lt. Col. J. Mitchell, 66th Ohio, 8/15/87, *B.P.* (3), 1507; Letter of Capt. William Alexander, 111th Pennsylvania, 9/2/87, *B.P.* (3), 1510-11.

4. *O.R.,* Part 1, 812; Gettysburg Newspaper Clippings Vol. 5, pp. 114-5, in Rock Creek, Vertical File 4-10, GNMP.

5. Lt. Col. John Nicholson, *Annual Reports of the Gettysburg National Military Park Commission 1893-1904* (Washington: Government Printing Office, 1905), 29, 38.

6. Ibid., 51.

7. Ibid., 59, 61-3.

INDEX

Baltimore Pike, 10, 11, 14ff, 20, 23, 28, 29, 54, 75, 76, 77, 79, 82, 84, 86, 89, 90, 126, 136
Benner (Christian) Farm, 35, 41
Benner's Hill, 16-18, 31, 32, 33, 34, 35, 37, 38, 39, 42, 139, 140
Breastworks (See Traverse), 44, 70, 129, 143

Candy, Col. Charles (Brigade) 26-7, 77, 79, 97ff, 102, 114, 137n.
Cobham, Col. George (Brigade), 26, 77ff, 147n.
Colgrove, Col. Silas, 23, 26-7, 82, 87, 89ff, 95, 126, 129, 131, 137n, 145n.
Confederate Regiments:
14th Louisiana, 60, 70, 105, 143
1st Maryland Battalion, 41, 51, 112, 114, 116, 139
1st North Carolina, 41, 65, 67, 86, 87, 112, 142, 146
3rd North Carolina, 41, 51, 63, 107, 112-3, 115, 139
53rd North Carolina, 108, 147
2nd Virginia, 87, 122, 145
5th Virginia, 116
10th Virginia, 41, 70-2, 109, 139
21st Virginia, 38
23rd Virginia, 67, 139, 142
25th Virginia, 19, 36, 42, 105
37th Virginia, 41, 67, 112
42nd Virginia, 38, 42
44th Virginia, 4, 58, 59, 141
48th Virginia, 59, 141
49th Virginia, 95, 146n.
50th Virginia, 35, 38
52nd Virginia, 95, 146

Culp's Hill (described), 17, 23-4

Daniel, Brig. Gen. Junius (Brigade), 105, 108-9, 112, 147n, 149n.

East Cemetery Hill, 10, 12, 14, 30, 35, 42, 157
Ewell, Lt. Gen. Richard, 13, 16ff, 29-30, 32, 27, 86, 105, 109, 122, 136n, 138n, 140n.

Federal Regiments:
5th Connecticut, 83
20th Connecticut, 26, 90, 97, 100, 109, 122, 144
27th Indiana, 26, 82, 92, 94, 95, 122, 126, 149
1st Maryland Eastern Shore, 146n.
1st Maryland Potomac Home Brigade, 27
3rd Maryland, 26
2nd Massachusetts, 26, 82, 83, 91, 92, 93, 94, 95, 97, 126, 149
107th New York, 26, 83, 89, 137, 144, 145
60th New York, 24, 27, 34, 35, 47, 56, 57, 58, 59, 141, 142, 148
78th New York, 24, 34, 55, 57, 141
123rd New York, 26, 66, 83, 112, 123, 125
137th New York, 24, 26, 54-5, 61, 64, 66-7, 69, 71-2, 74, 75, 124, 126, 141ff, 148, 149
145th New York, 26, 66, 83
147th New York, 70, 116, 142

151

About The Author

Though Yankee born and bred, historian John Archer dates his interest in the Civil War from his childhood discovery of Confederate ancestors on his family tree. He graduated from the University of Hartford where he received a B.A. in Psychology. John's first book, *"The Hour Was One of Horror" - East Cemetery Hill at Gettysburg,* is an interpretive guide to another little-understood area of the battle, and is available through Thomas Publications. He has also researched and written several articles for magazines specializing in the American Civil War. John now lives in Gettysburg with his wife Darlene, where he serves as a Licensed Battlefield Guide at Gettysburg National Military Park, and on staff at Gettysburg College.

15539618R00083

Made in the USA
Charleston, SC
08 November 2012